"As a web novice, Paula's book, *Pimp My Site*, feels like it was written just for me. Every web owner who wants to be taken seriously needs this helping hand."
Ian Ogilvy, actor, playwright, novelist

"Aside from being an excellent toolkit and handy resource, this book will make you see online marketing from all angles. There is something in here for beginners and more advanced users who may be lacking in certain areas. From search marketing right through to PR and optimisation, this book is a must have for anyone confronting the challenge of pimping a website."
Karen Hanton, MBE

"The one-stop-book for all things digital. It has everything you need to know about how to market your website. You can't go wrong here: easy to read, easy to understand and easy to implement."
Rachel Elnaugh, Entrepreneur, star of BBC TV's *Dragons' Den* and award winning Business Mentor

"Clear, easy-to-follow screen shots and instructions will guide you through each task to market, promote and optimise your website from beginning to end."
Caroline Marsh, Secret Millionaire

"As an entrepreneur in our digital age, I know how important the web is for getting the message out. When it comes to pimping your site at minimal cost, Paula's book shows the way! Highly recommended."
Toby Beresford, Syncapse

"Paula's book, *Pimp My Site,* has everything to optimise, promote and market a website. A novice's haven and a must have toolkit for web-savvy marketers."
Debbie Bird, Editor of *Babyworld*

"Crammed with useful, proven and easy to implement tips, *Pimp My Site* will be an indispensable asset for any business who needs to get 'out there'."
Jo Haigh, Bestselling Author of *The Business Rules*, *An Entrepreneur's Guide*, and *Tales from the Glass Ceiling* *in Business*

"The internet is a vast desert of missed opportunity punctuated with the occasional lush oasis of profit. If you want to thrive in this harsh landscape, better get yourself a map. Paula Wynne's book lays out a good guide for how to survive and prosper in the digital wilderness."
Clem Chambers, CEO of ADVFN.com and author of *The Armageddon Trade* and *The Twain Maxim*

"Paula Wynne's book, *Pimp My Site*, is a great start for small businesses if they cannot afford professional experts to do their digital marketing."
Anthony Quigley, Digital Marketing Institute

"Paula's excellent book covers everything you need to successfully promote your website. Keyword research, SEO, Pay Per Click, Social Networking, Email Marketing, Online PR etc. – it's all here in one handy digital marketing toolkit."
Ross Jackson, SEO and Search Consultant

Pimp My Site

YOUR DIY GUIDE TO SEO, SEARCH MARKETING, SOCIAL MEDIA AND ONLINE PR

PAULA WYNNE

CAPSTONE

Registered office

Capstone Publishing Ltd. (A Wiley Company), The Atrium, Southern Gate, Chichester, West Sussex, PO19 8SQ, United Kingdom

For details of our global editorial offices, for customer services and for information about how to apply for permission to reuse the copyright material in this book please see our website at www.wiley.com.

Library of Congress Cataloguing-in-Publication Data

9780857082428 (paperback), ISBN 9780857082503 (ebk),
ISBN 9780857082510 (ebk), ISBN 9780857082527 (ebk)

A catalogue record for this book is available from the British Library.

Set in 11.5/14 pt Adobe Caslon pro-Regular by Toppan Best-set Premedia Limited

Printed in TJ International Ltd, Padstow, United Kingdom

"The road to success is always under construction."
Anonymous

Contents

Acknowledgements

Thank you for picking up this book and I hope you enjoy reading it. By the end, you'll have a full Digital Marketing Strategy to optimise, promote and market your site. Firstly, I would like to say thanks to all the contributors and experts who have given up their time to offer you their best advice. And a special thank you to Karen Hanton for writing the Foreword.

Experts
Toby Beresford

Ross Jackson

Judith Lewis

Ian Dodson

Anthony Quigley

Dee Blick

Fiona Wright

Andrew Seel

Dan Fallon

Alex Johnson

A very special thank you to Iain, Jenny and the team at Wiley and Capstone for believing in *Pimp My Site* and being inspired to help bring this book to life.

I would also like to mention some of the special people in my life who have always supported my writing dreams!

My partner, Ken: you're a constant source of words, wit, smiles, laughter and strength.

My son, Kent: you have lived through my dream and I encourage you and Jane, Jack, Caydon, Cameron and Tanna and all your cousins to pursue your dreams with every ounce of energy and to always reach for the sky.

My Mom: you have always believed in me, a Mother's love sustains, builds and grows. Three people who are no longer with me, but I know they look down proudly: Penrose, Granny and Daddy. For my brothers and sisters and everyone in my family: for every dream we've ever dared to dream.

Foreword

When Paula asked me to write this Foreword, I wasn't sure what to expect. Many of my friends have read her first book, *Create A Successful Website*, and agree with me that it is excellent. On receipt of *Pimp My Site*, I was delighted to see the in-depth analysis of the chosen topics, which are broken down into 'Days' for easily working your way through the book.

I was brought up on a small farm in the North East of Scotland where we were used to making a little go a long way. This approach has stood me in good stead in my business life and one of the things I find really appealing about Paula's book is that it's all about things you can do for yourself. Paula's book sets out simple, easy-to-do ideas for creating a Digital Marketing Strategy which is a really refreshing change from so many over-complications in the digital world.

The book starts with the most fundamental aspect of website marketing – Keywords and Search Engine Optimisation (SEO). Here Paula shows how she has tackled this complex subject and dissected it bit by knobbly bit. Starting with the perception of what keywords are and how they affect your search marketing, Paula's knowledge and simple explanations make it understandable and enjoyable to know that you too can accomplish the mean feat of beating your competitors up the Google search ladder.

Moving on through SEO with On and Off Page Optimisation I was thrilled to see Paula's wide scope of techniques for new entrepreneurs to 'get found' by their visitors. She has woven all the tricks of the trade through her chapters and given them added potency with advice, comments and tips from her 'cherry-picked' experts.

They bring important and precious expertise to what could be dry and crusty topics and for which an agency would charge you a fortune! In one practical and versatile guide you have the author's experience relayed from a beginner's point of view as well as industry experts' talents. Nice.

Being a successful entrepreneur myself I know the value of a strong Digital Marketing Strategy. If a business is to achieve success in this area the subjects covered in this book, which range from SEO, Online Networking, PPC, Google Analytics, Blogging, Video and Article Marketing, Social Media and even Email Marketing, are all vital for Pimping One's Site.

Paula's engaging writing style will save many small businesses and digital marketers' time and money and she even gives you a full set of 'tools' for each theme she focuses on.

I enjoyed the PR chapters and here Paula's skill and expertise shine through – and I loved that she even has journalists involved by giving their own insider view of how to pitch to the media!

Aside from being an excellent toolkit and handy resource, this book will make you see online marketing from all angles. There is something in here for beginners and more advanced users who may be lacking in certain areas. From Search Marketing right through to PR and Optimisation, this book is a must have for anyone confronting the challenge of pimping a website.

In many respects, I wonder if we've only just come to the end of the beginning of internet marketing. Technology is again moving so fast, it's really exciting to imagine where we'll be at the end of another ten years.

Best wishes for Pimping Your Site!

Karen Hanton, MBE

Karen hails from the northeast of Scotland, but moved to London at the age of 18. After her initial training and career in HR, she became self employed at the age of 30. In October 2010 Karen sold her most recent venture toptable. com for $55 million.

Karen Hanton has received significant public recognition, including the *Financial Times* Moet Hennessy Extraordinary Achievers Award, and has been named as one of today's top 30 entrepreneurs in *New Business Magazine,* and one of the top 100 most influential people in the first decade of the internet in an NOP/e-consultancy poll. Karen was appointed MBE in the 2010 Birthday Honours.

Introduction

The idea for *Pimp My Site* was sparked from workshops I run to improve online site performance. The title and subjects within 'digital marketing' are so vital, and the content so jam-packed with so many juicy topics, rich features and essential elements for today's savvy marketers, they deserve to be on a book shelf. So *Pimp My Site* was born.

There are so many components to marketing and promoting a website. As we delve deeper into digital marketing (DM), your own digital marketing strategy (DMS) will start to form. At first it may seem vague with a scattergun approach, but don't worry, it may slowly evolve as your focus tightens and you button down your pimping hatches.

Whenever I refer to the term 'site' or 'website', this includes your business, organisation and association. In fact, it refers to anyone who wants and needs to encourage more traffic to their online web presence. If you work in a marketing or PR capacity, 'your site' will refer to your marketing role. 'Your site' also indicates your business or company.

I love teaching myself new things and I'm pleased to say that I am still learning – and I have learnt so much while researching deeper into digital marketing. Be proud to be a lifelong learner. I am! You have taken the first step in investing in your ongoing online education and I encourage you to continue this journey when you finish this book. Digital marketing is always changing and evolving and thus we all have to commit ourselves to constantly studying and learning new ways to promote, optimise and market our websites.

I have enjoyed every minute of my own digital marketing journey and with this book I want to motivate and inspire you to reach out and dip your toe into this dynamic and endlessly shifting tide!

How to Use the DIY Method

The book is broken down into bite-sized chunks using days instead of chapters. Each day gives you various topics, tasks and templates with easy-to-follow steps and colour visuals – the quickest way to understand without having to dissect all the geeky jargon.

Work It Baby, Work It

You might already be asking: "How on earth am I going to stick to this daily schedule?"

"Don't worry, you don't have to," is the simple answer. It is only there to guide you. You may want to do a few days in one go or you may feel compelled to race ahead and get it all done at once or dip back in whenever the need arises. You may even take many months to absorb and digest all that this book has to offer. Whatever your situation, use the daily schedule only as a working guide for the book's format.

Tip Watch

As well as quotes and examples, watch out for the following symbols that point to expert advice, top tips and jargon busters.

    Expert's quotes

    Tips and advice

    Jargon Buster

Resources

At the end of the book, you will find a list of useful resources that you can use to double check everything you have learnt and continue with further research and learning on particular topics.

Introducing Our Expert Panel

I have gathered a team of experts that every digital marketer and website owner would dream of having as an in-house team to guide them through setting up a strategy and being on hand to support them in every turn of their journey. These experts have generously agreed to share their business knowledge and online experience:

Toby Beresford

Ross Jackson

Ian Dodson

Judith Lewis

Anthony Quigley

Dan Fallon

Dee Blick

Andrew Seel

Alex Johnson

Fiona Wright

Get to know them by checking out their biographies and brief business summaries in the About the Expert Panel section starting on page 241.

Digital Is the New Black

The internet has changed the business world, pioneering a revolution from traditional to new online search marketing techniques. With it a whole new industry has emerged, which is literally taking the world by storm. New media agencies are setting up daily to help businesses convert from old marketing methods to new ones. Along with these ventures, new learning is bringing the majority of small businesses up to speed with online marketing.

Digital marketing is *the* way to market your business. The digital topics we'll investigate in this book will be:

- Search Engine Optimisation (SEO)
- Search Engine Marketing (SEM)
- Pay Per Click Advertising (PPC)
- Networking (Online)
- Social Media (SM)
- Online Media
- Blogging
- Bookmarking
- Internet Publicity
- Online PR
- Promotional Activities
- Email Marketing

Each subject has its own 'kit' with a magnetic set of tools for you to study, operate and cultivate. All of these topics will be explored over the coming chapters/days.

We are not going to be discussing telesales, print advertising, direct mail, printed brochures and trade shows or exhibitions in this book. Although offline or traditional marketing will still have an effect on your business, the results may be minimal and costly. We will focus on all things digital and discover how online marketing has taken over traditional marketing methods. Like me, I am sure you constantly marvel at how the internet has changed the world – the way we think, the way we find things, how we buy cool stuff on the net and how we have to think like our visitors to reach out to them.

So let's get cracking, and find out how to use digital marketing to pimp your site!

Day 1
Digital Marketing

Today you will learn:

- The basics of a digital marketing strategy
- How to build an audience persona
- Why you need to engage in search marketing
- How search engines work
- The difference between organic vs paid search marketing

So What Is Digital Marketing?

Digital marketing (DM) is selling, promoting and marketing your product or service online. One of our experts, Anthony Quigley, believes that digital marketing is now so fundamental in the marketing mix that people think about naming their company in terms of search expressions.

Digital marketing uses affordable digital channels and online tools, such as social media and email marketing. Most people start with Google when they need to browse, read, research, connect, join and buy, so you need to ensure potential visitors will find your product or service.

> **Ian Dodson on Digital Marketing**
>
> "Digital marketing is about what you need or want to market to your audience and relating that back to the audience and where to find them. Think of it this way – where are the people I need to talk to?"

Digital Marketing Strategy

So what do you do and how do you get started? Planning and delivering a digital strategy can be complex or really quite simple, depending on your objectives and targets. Most experts consider a digital marketing strategy (DMS) to be the process of planning, implementing and evaluating your vision and aspirations for your business or website. Elements that make up a full strategy will arise from your business or marketing plan or your online blueprint. Here I will cover the basics of a DMS and encourage you to read more and explore the subject in greater depth. The Digital Marketing Institute and many others offer their students a template and help them plan a full strategy.

> "Companies who are successful online are successful in different ways. Whereas companies who fail online, all fail in the same way."
>
> Ian Dodson, Digital Marketing Institute

Planning a Digital Marketing Strategy

When setting out the most effective route to market or 'pimping' your site's product or service, you need to decide on your goals, how to achieve them and how to promote your brand online. To keep things simple, I suggest that beginners to DM use a basic outline. As you grow in confidence and strength, and as your website shows improved KPIs (Key Performance Indicators), you can add to the plan and see it evolve, fatten and grow healthily to become a fully fleshed-out digital marketing strategy (DMS).

You may even need to create more detailed objectives to reach your main goal.

Basic Digital Marketing Strategy Template

Start with a structure to research and analyse your current site's situation:

1. Situation Analysis

2. Audience

3. Objectives

4. Channels

5. Action Plan

6. Budget

7. Measurement and Iteration

Let's take a quick look at each of these in turn.

1. Situation Analysis
This is where you get to understand yourself and your site and ask, "Where are we now?"

You may want to do an audit and SWOT analysis to gauge customers and competitors. It would be good to include trends and industry sectors.

SWOT: This analysis is a calculated way to plan and evaluate the Strengths, Weaknesses, Opportunities, and Threats involved in your online business.

2. Audience

Next you should evaluate and understand your customer or client who starts out as a visitor. A clear understanding of your target audience(s) will impact all aspects of your campaign, marketing media used, channel, message, layout and structure and content, right down to the words and language you use to describe what you do.

If you have several different audiences, such as B2B or B2C, rank them in order of importance and break down the categories further. You may have existing clients as well as future or prospective customers to flesh out, and you could possibly be talking to both B2B and B2C audiences.

For example, iHubbub's business audience ranges from professional consumers who work from home, home-based businesses, journalists who want to use our site as a portal to get information on the home working world, to sponsors and corporate companies who want to reach this audience for showcasing their products and recruiters who may want to get their projects outsourced. So you should segment your audience down several layers to define each persona that you want to reach, albeit in different ways. Then allocate resources accordingly as you may not have time and 'bodies' to look after each audience. Once you understand your audience's expectations and goals, you are better suited to prioritise which ones you will tackle first.

Character Building

Experts often refer to 'being in your visitor's shoes' as building a 'persona', almost like an author would build a fictional character. A creative writing or screen-writing course will teach a new writer how to create a skeleton or bio of a character and then add meaty character traits to outline a whole, 3D, fully-formed personality.

For your DMS, you too will form a persona with human needs and behaviour in order to recognise who your customer, visitor or client is, what they do and where they go to make online decisions and purchases. Just as an author would give their character a home, you too will designate geographical locations for your personas. In some cases, this will be more relevant.

 My Top Tip

If your business has a local base, regional office or national HQ, you need to reflect these locations.

Persona

Brainstorm your persona or use mind mapping techniques to fatten your persona's torso. Try some of these ideas:

- Age
- Educational stage
- Experience level
- Technical, mechanical or industrial ability
- Online aptitude
- Relationship position
- Financial status
- Products they buy
- Publications they read
- Where they network, such as Twitter, LinkedIn or Facebook
- Channels they visit, for example their favourite TV channel or radio station

Digital Space

If you were to draw a large circle or pie chart to find where this 'persona' goes for making decisions about purchases, Google will most likely take up most of the pie with YouTube following closely on its tail along with other search engines. Networking sites, such as Facebook and social media platforms, gobble another chunky slice of your pie – all of which will be discussed in the coming chapters of this book.

3. Objectives

Set goals and objectives for your digital campaigns. You may even need to create more detailed objectives to reach your main goal. Bear the following in mind:

Specific: get down to the nitty gritty with a calendar timetable

Measurable: have systems in place to accurately track your campaigns and stay on target. This way you will experience the excitement of achievement, which will motivate and urge you to reach your goal

Attainable: the actions to influence this outcome are under your control, so plan your steps and create a time frame. Start a list and tick each activity as you go

Realistic: be reasonable about how long it will take to achieve the goals set and include rewards or little treats when you reach different milestones

Timed: set a deadline for delivering on the objectives with a trackable date. By doing this you will set your mind into gear, and without you being aware, it will be quietly working away at reaching the goal date. Setting a time also cunningly gives you a sense of urgency to ensure you keep making progress.

My Top Tip

Break your main objective down into smaller ones. When I set an objective to make my first book an Amazon bestseller, I had several other goals to help me reach this high target, such as several different ways to reach potential readers.

4. Channels

A channel is a 'route to market'. This means the different channels and methods of reaching your target audience and where you detail the activities.

Include the following in your digital marketing mix:

- Keywords and search engine optimisation
- Search engine marketing, Pay Per Click
- Marketing and online display advertising
- Online marketing including blogs, eBooks and articles
- Video broadcasting
- Social networking and social media
- PR and publicity campaigns
- Email marketing

Judith Lewis' Top Tip

Like in search, social mentions rank better for people who comment, 'like' and 'link' more often or engage with a social media profile.

5. Action Plan

How do you implement this strategy? Start by defining and establishing the who, what, when, where, how and how much. Make prolific notes on activities you can do and, as you go through each section of the book, scribble away to your heart's content. All new thoughts are creative so use them as food for thought and then strengthen each idea with research and nail down who is the best person to implement the activity (internal and external resources), exactly what you will do, when you will do it, where it will be done, how you intend to get all the elements organised and controlled and how much it will cost.

6. Budget

Get costs and quotes for your activities and then decide on your budget. Remember that your budget can go up or down during your campaigns so if you work for yourself there doesn't have to be a fixed cost. However, having one or at least a budgeting goal will help establish how quickly you can get your DMS working to pimp your site.

"You can never have too much money for a Digital Marketing Strategy so take bite-sized chunks to find what's best for your site."

Ian Dodson, Digital Marketing Institute

7. Measurement and Iteration

How will you know your DMS has worked? There are excellent online tools to track, analyse and measure your social media campaigns. Do the same for each activity in the channels you choose. For example, if you are doing a PR campaign you can decide to pay for a PR monitoring service or you can track this via Google Alerts at no charge and keep a record of any press clippings.

It is also advisable to work out a Return on Investment (ROI), in order to establish which campaigns work best and why. This will inevitably help your future plans from both a cost and budgeting point of view and a success ratio for activities you undertake.

Set up KPIs (Key Performance Indicators), which help to identify and quantify key areas of your website as the best or worst performers. Think of your KPIs as the heartbeat of your site: they will indicate how your online business is growing, what areas are weak and need more work and which are strong and robust. This information will also show you what opportunities lie ahead. If you run reports in fancy graphs, they will quickly and clearly show you how well your site is performing and where to focus your energy. Try setting up graphs in Excel or PowerPoint to monitor your traffic, your products, different services, your revenue and any other important indicators of success.

Your Ongoing Digital Marketing Strategy

So, as you take your first steps towards creating your DMS by exploring search engines and how people search, make notes at the end of each day and by the end of the book your DMS should be crystal clear. It can be a daunting task – and I know this because I have been there and felt that I was drowning in a digital sea of marketing methods. Like me, I have no doubt that you too will be rejuvenated by the excitement and vitality of this new marketing medium.

The importance of a successful DMS is to understand what works for your site and reiterate your successes. Always optimise all campaigns because the result is traffic, which in turn drives visitor behaviour and ultimately expansion of your site. Best of all, you will get a huge buzz when you see your site growing. It is also great fun and highly satisfying when you see the graph on a steep upward climb, especially if you have taught yourself from scratch. Be proud to show off your growth!

Search Marketing

Search engine marketing (SEM) is the combination of Search engine optimisation (SEO) and Pay Per Click (PPC) advertising. SEO is the process of improving ranking in search engine results by making optimisation changes to your website. PPC, on the other hand, is an online advertising tool in which advertisers pay their host in advance. It is

 SEARCH ENGINE OPTIMISATION: SEO is the process of improving your search ranking in search engine results. SEO is how 'search' ranks and delivers results.

possible to be top of the ranking immediately with 'paid for advertising'. However, to achieve this and to remain on top of the list can become costly.

"Promote your organisation by attracting people to your website through search engines."

Ross Jackson, Ross Jackson Consultancy

Your site is found by search engines in several ways: by submission to the search engines and link building and getting search engines to find you through optimisation and social media links. My experience has shown that the correct use of SEO can bring in phenomenal results to a start up or new business. As a result, I have concentrated the next two Days on keywords and optimisation, which is broken down into on-page optimisation and off-page optimisation (link building).

"Search and social media are coming together. Each one has an effect on the other. For brand exposure, awareness and sales, the whole package together is more valuable than individual parts."

Judith Lewis, Beyond

LINK BUILDING: Pump up your website's popularity by building links. Link building is important as search engines are known to trust websites with lots of high-quality incoming links. The most valuable links come from relevant websites which are already trusted by search engines.

SEM is now the fastest growing form of advertising, and because of the complexities many companies rely on agencies to manage their search marketing. Advertisers spend billions in digital advertising, so I have included a separate chapter on search marketing tools, where we cover Pay Per Click (PPC).

The largest providers are Google, Yahoo! Search Marketing and Microsoft's Adcentre. SEM is often run in conjunction with SEO. An SEO strategy can take up to six months or longer to take full effect so you may want to implement an SEM campaign to ensure you appear in the results of the search while your SEO gets going.

My Top Tip

Think of SEO and SEM as the hare and the tortoise: SEO is the tortoise that sets a steady pace and doesn't give up until it gets to the winning post, which is the pole position in Google. SEM is the PPC hare who darts up front, leaving the tortoise behind, determined to be first and beat competitors. The hare may, or may not, take a break (depending on budget), but it rests on the sidelines in Google's right 'paid for' column, while the tortoise overtakes and becomes Google's No.1.

Whichever you decide to do, the first few Days will cover each aspect in greater detail to ensure your toolbox is fully equipped.

Search Engines

Search engines search the entire internet for content using keywords that people use to search for something, now fondly known as 'Googling'.

My Top Tip

Think of a search engine as a giant spider (yuck) crawling across a garden in search of bugs, mites or anything edible.

When potential visitors enter a keyword or key phrase into the search box, a results page pops up instantly, ranking pages in order of their relevance to the keywords used.

The Main Search Engines

The three main search engines use different techniques to rank websites. Of course, there are plenty of others, but we'll just chat about the 'biggies'.

Google
Google checks the quality and relevance of the content. It also checks links coming back to your site from other sites. You will find Google's Webmaster Tools in your account so learn how they assess your site.

Yahoo!
Yahoo! began as a web directory, but it also offers link analysis tools so check out their SEO articles.

"What we do socially is now reflected in search results."

Judith Lewis, Beyond

Bing

Formerly known as MSN, Microsoft's search engine, Bing, will rank your website on the page content and how relevant it is to the keywords used. Like Google, it also ranks according to the number of quality sites linking back to you.

So, at a glance you can see how significant it is to have 'relevant and specific' keywords on each page in order to be optimised by these industrious and clever guys.

How Search Engines Work

Search engines use software programs, called spiders, robots or crawlers, to search the internet. These programs build an index, database or directory of the internet, providing a complex web of links, pages, keywords, descriptions, metadata and more. Remember the yucky garden spider. It will know where damp logs harbour grubs and bugs. Their 'index' directory is by no means comparable to web crawlers, but the idea is the same.

Index: This content and source code is then analysed and indexed according to the titles, content, headings or meta tags you have used. The search engines will find your pages, and millions of others in 0 to 30 seconds, Mach 4!

Query: The data is stored in order to be quickly accessible when someone types a search question into a search engine.

Cache: Google stores each word in every page it finds (imagine the storage size!). You may have seen Google giving you a 'cached' or copied page in a search result, look out for this.

 ORGANIC OR SPONSORED?

Sponsored links are usually on the right-hand side of search pages but sometimes at the top of the left side, often on lightly shaded backgrounds. Companies pay Google Adwords and others to be featured here.

An **organic search** is always on the left-hand side and reflects Google's ranking in importance to relevant keywords. On some occasions there may be a couple of paid results above the organic list, as mentioned above.

We'll go through ways of submitting your site to the various search engines so you can get indexed and we are going to tackle keywords, how to find them and the best way to use them.

Domain vs URL

The difference between a domain name and a URL is that the domain name stops with the .com or .co.uk, etc, whereas the URL is the whole web address, including everything after the .com.

For example, www.remoteemployment.com/about-remote-employment.aspx is about our site, while our news page URL will be www.remoteemployment.com/news. This gives search engines an inkling of what the page is about.

> **Judith Lewis on 'Search'**
>
> We have evolved to an age of page titles, descriptions, URLs, site links, video, news, recent results, images, blogs, shopping results, and more – all being fed directly into the search results in response to a user query.
>
> This means that the Tweet you just put out could pop up in the search results for your company right now in a social search.
>
> That image you uploaded to Flickr could now be ranking you or your company's name.

Organic vs Paid Search Marketing

There are several benefits to being listed in the organic results on Google, which is the left-hand side of the search results. The most important benefits are:

- *No cost* – your hard work is all it costs for being highly ranked
- *More traffic* – most people know the difference between the paid results on the right and the organic links on the left and will invariably click those first
- *Traffic jam* – because search spiders crawl your site regularly they check and maintain your rank, which allows more people to find you before your competitors.

My Top Tip

Ensure your page content matches the relevant keywords for your subject matter.

Since Remote Employment became Google's No 1 for its primary keywords, we found that our other keywords soon marched up the ladder. As a result, we are found by more working professionals who want alternative ways to work. And they find us from a wide variety of keywords.

Just to be sure you know the difference between organic and sponsored results, see the following diagram, which reflects how Google produces search results. Top left is the place you want to be with a natural search! An organic search is always on the left-hand side and this reflects Google's ranking in importance to relevant keywords.

Sponsored results are on the right-hand side and sometimes on top of the left side. Companies pay to be featured here. The top sponsored adverts above the organic list are the best performers based on their ad rank and quality score. In this search I typed in 'social networking'.

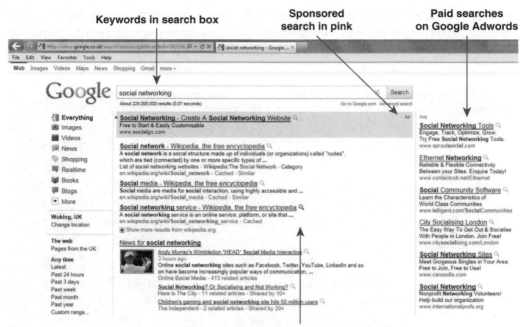

Keywords in search box   Sponsored search in pink   Paid searches on Google Adwords

This area is organic or natural search results

How to Find You?

First and foremost, you have to work out what words, phrases and one-liners people will use to find your site. Even if you go for a free website or can only afford a small pay-monthly site without all the bells and whistles, you can still get to the top of Google's ladder with carefully constructed content pages containing strategically placed keywords and phrases. Just as Peter Pan blew magic dust over Wendy before they flew off to Neverland, you too can sprinkle some Google dust through your site and watch the Google magic!

Google's Golden Triangle

According to Mediative Performance LP (formerly Enquiro Search Solutions Inc), the results of this eye-tracking study prove that, just as the famed Bermuda Triangle traps wayward travellers, there is a 'golden triangle' on Google that 'traps' users' eyeballs. The golden triangle, clearly seen in this screenshot, is a triangle-shaped viewing pattern that reaches out from the top left of the search results page. The golden triangle includes the top three organic search results.

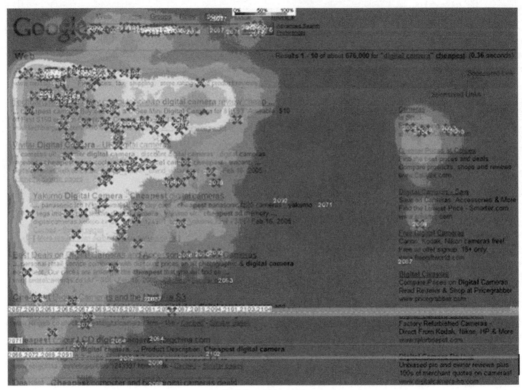

Golden Triangle

Enquiro believes that user 'eyeball-scanning' drops off dramatically after this, with only 50 percent of users moving on to the second page of search results. Most people won't trawl through pages and pages of results to find what they are looking for. You can see the 'eyeball heat' in the triangle shown in this screenshot.

Enquiro suggests that internet searchers have a collection of words in their heads that are more than just the query terms they type into the search field. They will subconsciously scan for these words in the search results. This collection of words (in their head) will include other related terms that are relevant to what they are searching in the first place.

> **My Top Tip**
>
> Read more about Google's Golden Triangle here:
>
> www.enquiro.com/enquiro-develops-googles-golden-triangle.php

Summary

Most people start with Google when they need to browse, read, research, connect, join and buy, so you need to ensure potential visitors will find your product or service. You will start becoming aware of how digital marketing makes use of digital channels and online tools to help you sell, promote and market your product or service online.

While a digital marketing strategy (DMS) is the method you use for planning, implementing and evaluating your vision and aspirations for your business or website, the elements that make up a full strategy will arise from your business or marketing plan or your online blueprint. Although planning and delivering a digital strategy can be complex, it can also be a simple plan and this largely depends on your objectives and targets.

Today we also discovered the difference between organic or natural results versus paid or sponsored listings. Understanding, even in the simplest way, how search engines work, gives you an idea of the complexities behind keywords and search engine marketing. In the next few Days we will slowly unearth just how easy it can be to rank high on Google and we'll break down the myth that search engine marketing is a complex art attempted only by the lion-hearted!

Now is the time to shift the way you think about your site. Desperation and running around like a headless chicken comes from fear. Fear of 'not knowing' what to do and how to do it. The more you work on pimping your website to make it a success, the more excited and empowered you will become.

Visualise the goals you set today for your DMS with a clarity of vision and an intensity that makes you believe you will achieve them. This will enrich your digital marketing experience and fuel the passion you already harbour for your site. In turn, it will energise you to optimise, promote and market your site, turning it into a Google magnet and a beehive of success (aka traffic jam).

So, before we go any further, put your hand on your heart and solemnly promise to use all the information and learning in this book to improve your website. Make an immediate and long-lasting commitment to constantly use the tools herein to create an impelling, effectual and powerful digital marketing strategy to pimp your site.

Day 2
Keywords

Today you will learn:

- How to use keywords effectively
- Which keywords are primary
- How to set up a keyword strategy
- Where to use primary and secondary keywords
- Why keyword placement is imperative to being found by search engines

What Are Keywords?

Keywords are the most essential ingredients to ensure your site will be visible and indexed on search engines. Using them correctly and effectively will drive potential clients or customers to your site. Without strategic keyword placement, your site will be a mish-mash of gobbledy-gook to the search engines.

Your main objective is to be high up the organic results. When we venture on to On Page Optimisation in Day 3, you will find out why keywords are taking over our lives. More important is knowing how to use them to maximise your search marketing. Keywords will also come into play if you decide to do Google Adwords or any PPC campaigns and we will chat more about that in Day 5. To build a search-engine friendly site, your first step is researching the best keywords to suit your site.

> *"Keywords should turn searchers into visitors, and visitors into customers."*
> Ross Jackson, Ross Jackson Consultancy

It is not a case of ad hoc-ing any old words that come to mind into your pages and hoping it works. It is a complex business, but one that is easily learned and achieved by even the most extreme novice. Before I started my own business, I had no idea how to find the right keywords as I was able to employ agencies to do this for me. The key point here: your keywords need to be specific and relevant to your product or service and also to the content on each page of your site.

Leverage Your Niche

Without realising it, when we launched Remote Employment, one problem we had was the high level of competition within our niche.

When we discovered we had to fight our way through the toughest and most competitive keywords in the world, we thought we faced an impossible task. Especially because we didn't have the skill or expertise in-house to get this done and we had limited budget to outsource to an agency. Thus, we had a steep learning curve ahead of us. It is not impossible to rank for high-end keywords, but you have to start small and target long-tail keywords (see below) before tackling the big players.

The only way we could do this was by opening up our content to viewers as well as search engines. We couldn't do this overnight, or even within months for that matter, so we started to optimise our resource and article pages. This meant writing highly targeted pages that focused on specific long-tail keywords. This ended up being our saviour!

Long-Tail Keywords

Long-tail keywords are three to five keywords strung together to form a long phrase. To be used effectively, they should be highly relevant and precise to your product or service. Ideally, you should also go through your list of main keywords and look at them from a different angle and put a different emphasis on a particular keyword each time.

In our case, our main keywords were extremely competitive: 'working from home' or 'working at home'. So, if it was going to be like walking through a minefield to get up the Google ladder for this keyword phrase, how could we use it to be more specific and relevant to our site? (Notice that I'm repeating myself with 'relevant and specific' – for good reason.)

We have jobs, right? They are working at home and remote working jobs, correct? Okay, so how about optimising 'working from home' with the word 'jobs' in front or behind? Sounds like it might work? Now, how about being more specific and even more relevant? We don't post any jobs that are not flexible. So, to create an even better long-tailed keyword, we started optimising 'flexible home based jobs' and 'flexible home based jobs working from home'. See the long tails forming? Quite a mouthful you may say. And I agree. But it worked.

You see, when your visitors use a highly specific search phrase, they tend to be looking for exactly what they are actually going to buy (or in our case not to buy, but to apply for jobs). They wanted flexible jobs and work from home jobs so by combining the two into one long-tail phrase we ended up killing two keywords with one stone. We became Google's No 1 for both 'flexible jobs' and 'home based jobs'. In the world, I might add.

Judith Lewis' Top Tip

Conversions are higher on phrases of 3 to 5 words so don't just target 1 to 2 word combinations.

It seems pretty mad to think that a small business like ours could beat the huge temping agencies that have been around for donkey's years by using the phrase 'flexible jobs'. We were astounded to discover we had cracked this on a global scale. Anyone searching anywhere in the whole world for a 'flexible job' would find us first in the 'organic' list (organic being natural and not paid results). What fun – I did say this could be enjoyable!

My point is to show you how we shot up the Google ladder with long-tails. In virtually every case, such specific searches are far more likely to convert to sales, registrations or sign ups. You, too, can create long-tail keywords if your keywords are niche and competitive.

The more niche and more focused your keywords the better. By the time their fingers hit the keyboard, a person's mind is already set. They subconsciously go through a thought pattern before searching and they don't even realise that they are using long-tail keywords. For example, people used to type in 'buy a car', and moved to 'Ford car'. Then 'buy a Ford car' or 'buy a Ford Focus car' and now they use 'buy a Ford Focus car in Bracknell'. Adding an area to your long tail is particularly important if you have a location based business.

In the next two screenshots, you will see I have searched for 'social networking community sites UK' and then 'social networking community sites US'. Notice that this renders almost completely different results:

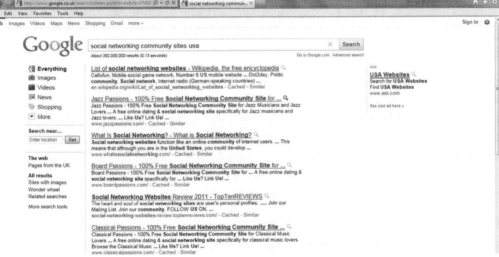

Note: The UK results show more than 62 million in 0.15 seconds whereas the US results were 392 million in 0.13 seconds.

Knowing What Keywords to Use

In one of my SEO workshops, I had a lady who was helping her husband optimise his site and she told me that when she typed in certain words that reflected her business name, their site was in first place. When we discussed what the site was and what keywords she was using, it was clear that the keywords she typed were not the type of phrases anyone else on the course would use. She was using a direct description of their business.

Think about it this way: if you type in a search for 'remote employment' you will find Remote Employment's website at number one. But people who don't know that such a site with that particular name exists will not type the phrase 'remote employment' as a search phrase. Therefore, we have to find keywords that people will type, such as home working, remote working, home-based jobs, etc. We then optimise those particular words so people can find the site.

The same applies to you. I would not necessarily type in the same words that you would use to describe your site. We all think differently (thank goodness) so use a wide range of potential words. I helped a training company that was not being found and thus not achieving ranking or traffic. I quickly discovered that the words they used to describe their service were not words that a typical browser would type into a search box.

For example, the phrase 'secrets of a successful website' is unlikely to be the set of keywords you would enter if you wanted to find how to create a successful website. You would possibly use 'how to start a website', 'starting up a website', 'website start up', 'setting up an internet business' and so on. The search term 'secrets of a successful website' may be found if that was my website's name and if I had fully optimised it for those words. I would have to find other words that people will use and then optimise those words in order to be found.

You need to establish what kind of words a potential visitor would use when trying to find your site. This is the key 'secret of success' to optimising your site.

In Your Buyer's Shoes

Many web owners fall down in this area, as I have done. Every click, visit and analytical stat originates from human visitors so it is imperative that you delve into how they think and feel. Okay, there are robots and software scouring the net that also use clicks, but I am talking about clicks that will make a difference to your site if they buy from you or engage with you in some way. Spend some time getting to know as much as you can about your prospective new browsers. Imagine all the possible words they could use to find your site.

Try brainstorming different words and even ask friends and family around for a finger buffet and then pick their brains. Ask them what they would use to find your product or service and you will get a wide range of words that people use to search for a particular kind of site. Even make a game of it if necessary. The top words, most words, or best niche combinations wins. Then, type in those keywords and see where you rank. You can also type any keywords you think are relevant to your site and then find what words your competitors use. This will give you an idea that you may not be found by people who use those particular words until you optimise the site for those words.

As I was growing up, my mother always made me consider an argument in someone else's shoes. It drove me mad, but one day her words knocked me on the head and made me realise I should be doing the same for my keywords.

> *"Get a descriptive, keyword-rich domain name. Google favours these domains in its rankings for searches based on those exact words."*
>
> Ross Jackson, Ross Jackson Consultancy

Keep that in mind and write content that ensures your customers' priorities are met quickly by guiding them with effective use of your keywords, prominently featured on your home page and other primary landing pages.

Using Keywords Effectively

We all describe and phrase things in different ways. The words you are planning to use in your online business may be different from the words your customers use. One of the hotels I worked for used all sorts of industry jargon that I, as a newcomer, had to get to grips with. So how could we begin to make our guests understand it? We had to break these down to simple search terms in order to get the website found for different areas of the hotel business, such as accommodation, restaurant, spa, etc. Similarly, we had to target each page's key message and make those keywords work hard. Just as a hotel has different areas of keywords, so your product range may differ so broadly that each set of keywords is different.

Be sure you don't fall into the 'wordy' trap. In other words, use simple, clear and concise text to express what you do and what that particular page is about.

The Three-Click Rule

A useful way to test the effectiveness of your keywords is to make sure your visitors can get to where they want to go on your site within three quick, easy-to-find clicks. Your keywords can help your visitors walk down an easy path in the three-click rule and get to their destination point quickly.

For example, if I want new iHubbub visitors to get to the membership page super fast, I would have a keyword text link on the home page, which leads to a page all about memberships, what they offer and the benefits to the visitor (remember that they are still only a visitor at this stage). And then one final (third) link to the actual sign-up page so they hop across '3' links to get to where I want them to convert from a visitor to a member. This link again would use the relevant keywords in the text link. It shouldn't be 'Sign up here' or 'Click here to sign up'. Instead it should read something like 'Sign up now to join the [my keywords follow] home business network'.

The destination point depends on your objective for that particular page. More than likely it will be the 'Order' or 'Check Out' page, but it could also be a newsletter sign-up, membership registration or special offers. Your example may be any one of these or even to check out your latest products or news. So use the following questions to ask what words you would use in your potential client's shoes:

- What will they want to know about your offering?
- What will they gain from visiting your site?
- How will it benefit them?
- What is your website really all about?
- What will your adverts shout about?

- What are they searching for?
- Why should they be coming to you and not your competitors?
- Do they want value for money?

Consider Your Questions from a Male and Female Perspective
- Will they take a tactical approach?
- Will they have an emotional or impulsive reaction?
- Will their decision be carefully thought out and planned long in advance?
- Will techno jargon tick their box?

Consider Your Questions from an Age Perspective
- Is your audience primarily younger? If so, how do they think and feel about products or services similar to yours?
- If your audience is older, what processes would they possibly go through to get to a decision about products or services similar to yours?
- Younger visitors are more likely to be turned on by cool tools.
- Older visitors may be more conservative and consider all options.

Think Like Your Visitors

Mastering keywords begins with understanding how to think like the visitors to your site. They may think of different keywords to type into Google, so you need to brainstorm every possibility to ensure you catch them all in your keyword net. If you could get into their minds (or shoes) what words or search phrase would you be typing into a search box? Consider what words they use, not the words or jargon you know and therefore assume that they would use.

Then you have to refine those words to get the best ones so you don't stuff your site with any words that may suit you. That would be like entering the danger zone. Instead, you'll work out a Keyword Strategy and then tailor all your chosen keywords to your site's pages, to ensure you are found for these words.

Where do you start and what do you do? We'll break this segment down into smaller chunks, but as I've said before, start with your visitors and learn to understand how they search and how they would describe your service.

Write for Your Audience

Your research will give you all the best words and phrases on a given topic, and the keyword tools you'll pick up in Day 3 will help you find the ones that people use most often.

Earlier on, you walked in your visitors' shoes and by now you know how they think, what they react to, and what type of buying language they speak.

Don't run the risk of spoiling great copy by trying to write for the search engines. Forget about them for the time being and write for your target audience.

Remember this Quick Page Checklist
- What is the page about?
- Who is it for?
- Do you have multiple audiences?
- Attract and engage your visitors.
- Gain their confidence to sell your products.
- Call to action with three clicks.

Your keywords will guide you to write content that provides the majority of potential buyers with a wide range of interesting topics.

Now, as we move on to how to work with keywords, keep your content creative and show your passion and imagination. Don't smother your copy with keywords and thus ruin your chances of having your visitors return again and again because of boring copy.

Remember, it's a balancing exercise. A general rule of thumb is to keep repeating variations of your keywords. Horrid, I know, but get used to it now, accept it as the new way to write for a website and get on with it.

Keyword Strategy

Your keyword strategy is neverending. You will be constantly monitoring and evaluating certain words, adding new ones and manipulating the ones that are lagging behind. Set yourself quarterly targets. This will act as a prompt to assess which keywords need a boost, which need the boot and to include any new ones that have come to light.

How to Work with Keywords

When you write for the people who visit your site, keep in mind that it is best to optimise a page for a few keywords, rather than too many phrases. Focus optimisation on a primary and secondary keyword phrase for each page. If you try to optimise for too many, you may end up diluting the effectiveness of the most important keywords and thus none of them will rank well. You know what it's like when you spread yourself too thin and juggle too many tasks, trying to do too many things at once. You end up NOT getting one thing done properly.

The same applies to your page. That key message on your page may also be spread too thinly if too many different keywords water down the page's relevance to specific keywords. Groan. I know – *those* words again (relevant and specific), but I am sure by now you can see the importance of being relevant and specific on every page.

Recipe for Keyword Success

Keyword Relevance: Start by choosing a page and decide on your target keywords for the content on that page. Just as you would set aside a recipe of ingredients for a special meal, have your keyword research to hand.

Headline Keywords: If you're baking a cake, your key ingredients would be flour and eggs, so add important keywords to headers, sub-headers and links.

Intro Keywords: As you would add other ingredients to your dish, use the most important keywords in the page title and preferably high up in the first paragraph.

Keyword Placement: When you're prepping your special meal, you check to see everything is in order before popping it in the oven. Same here. Check your copy to ensure you have placed keywords on your page and carefully woven them throughout the page. Let the content flow naturally and effortlessly, making sure that it still reads well with the inclusion of your keywords.

Page Layout: Mix your keywords through a simple and good-looking page layout. Make it easy for people to read and your page will rise to the occasion and work for the search engines as well. As you start getting familiar with keywords, have a visual image in mind of where you could use keywords, as seen in the following screenshot. It also creates a mental picture of the most important placement areas on your page for keywords. We'll go through the ideal page structure and keyword placement in greater detail in Day 4.

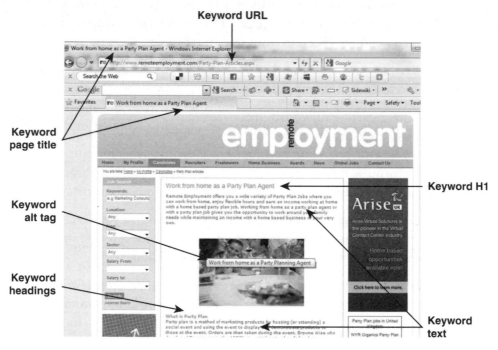

For example, I optimised the words 'party plan agent'. This page went from 0 to Google's page 1 in 60 seconds . . . okay, so I'm fibbing on the 60-seconds bit, but it was super fast. I wanted to ensure more people found our party planning clients so I optimised this page and forgot about it. When I looked a couple of weeks later, there it was, at the top of the ladder!

Key Places to Use Your Keywords

Here is a checklist for the most important places to feature your keywords:

URL: Each page on your website will have its own URL (Universal Resource Locator, normally generated from the page title). Most CMS software allows you to create page URLs, so use that page's keywords in your URL. This screenshot shows where to find keywords in your browser.

The Title: Your page title is vitally important and should include your primary keywords or phrase – more on this tomorrow with SEO. In the meantime, see the screenshot below, which shows you the title keywords in a Google search result.

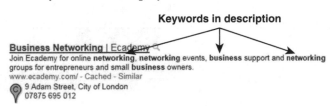

Headings and Sub-Headers: Also known as H1 Tags, the <h> tags that are used throughout your content pages should contain keywords. So the heading 'Our New Jobs' is weak, whereas 'New Home Based Jobs' is far better.

The Description: Your page description should include the search term. It will be the first text that a search engine encounters. From the following screenshot, you'll see how keywords are displayed in the search results in bold words.

Body Copy: By now you should understand what your keyword phrases are and use them in natural language on your pages. Weave them through different topics, sentences and text. Sprinkle them wherever you can, as often as you can, but don't stuff them down a search engine's throat!

Hyperlinks: The words or phrase used in hyperlinks tell your visitors and the search engine what your page is all about. Be clever and use this in links to other websites and on internal links to pages within your own site. Don't ever use 'click here'. Instead find a term such as 'home workers'.

Tags: These are rich words or phrases used to describe your site's pages to visitors and the search engines. Tags come in different forms, the main ones being metatags (covered in Day 4) and tags that are added to pages to flag content of interest. This is often used on community sites, such as the new social network, iHubbub, that I have been developing while writing this book.

Alt Tags: Check the page layout image on page 30 which shows how your alt tag is displayed when a mouse hovers over an image. Inside your CMS admin area there will be a place to upload images and include alt tags. Now take a look at the following screenshot to see how to include the image's alt tag with primary keywords.

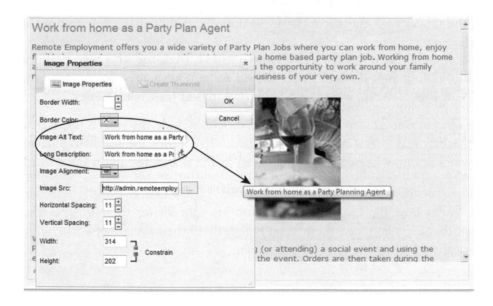

This will then populate your images on site with a brief keyword-rich description of the image for accessibility purposes, as well as help search engines to understand what your image is about. Remember Google's spiders and crawlers can't see pretty pictures, but they will gobble up the alt tag.

WYSIWYG: This stands for 'What You See Is What You Get' and is an editing application for creating and editing websites.

Your admin will more than likely differ, but there should be a place to add an alt tag. It is normally in image properties, in your WYSIWYG editor or try right clicking on the image while you're in admin. If you can't find it, ask your hosted software supplier or developer.

More Places to Feature Keywords

Keep the keywords flowing in other places throughout your site and always be aware of what you are writing about to ensure you are using those precious words. It will increase your Google Juice!

Link Title: Use keywords in your hyperlinks and use the title to embed your keywords into your page. This can also be used to link to another page in your site or to link to another site. This is best used in building strong internal links within your own site.

Bulleted Lists: Add or repeat keywords in a list. This not only breaks up blocks of text on a page, making it easier for scan readers but at the same time offers you the chance to make some of your keywords stand out.

Quotes: Quotations or short, quick speech extracts are another way to repeat meaningful words.

Interviews: If you run a site that features articles or reviews and you interview people, use the Q&As to impact strong keyword phrases.

Link Swaps: Building and swapping links with other sites is a great way to promote your site and get extra traffic. When you swap links ask for specific linking text to be used. Whenever I swap links for Remote Employment I send them details of what I would like them to use for my links, namely the link, the keywords and the headline – you will see an example of this when we discuss link building later on in this section.

Article References: A resource box at the bottom of an article is a way to reinforce your keywords by mentioning all the links and resources covered in the body copy – yet another way to repeat essential words.

Summary: If your site features an article area, you may have an intro or summary box. Repeat primary words to describe the article.

Testimonials: It's a good idea to carry a testimonial page to show how wonderful your site is, so it's an even better idea to use keywords in the quotes. See ours here: www.remoteemployment.com/Employers-Testimonials.aspx. I haven't tried this, but you could write a testimonial suggestion to make it easier for them and at the same time it helps you to get the right keywords into your testimonials.

Press Releases: We'll discuss this more on Day 10, but do keep in mind that linking text in your press releases is a great way to use keywords. These feature in your news pages and on other sites that use your release, thus bringing visitors back to your site.

Published Articles: When you submit an article to another site, you should be able to specify a blurb or one-liner about you and your site so use this for deliberate placing of keywords. It will also gain Google Juice points, which we will cover in link building.

Email Signature: This is obviously not on your website, but another excellent way to bring awareness about your company image and brand is to use keywords in your email signature. Along with your logo, same font and colour scheme, your tagline or slogan you can string a crafty one-liner of keywords so anyone receiving your email 'gets' your site concept in a snap. For example, with Remote Employment I add to my company email signature, 'We champion remote and home working'. For iHubbub I would use something like 'The home business social network'. Can you spot the long tail keyword here?

Keyword Traps

Intentional overuse of keywords, or 'keyword stuffing', not only creates text that could earn a penalty from search engines, which you cannot afford, but it also turns people off your site.

There is something called 'Black Hat', which refers to devious ways to influence search engine indexes. For example, some sites use hidden text on pages and have keywords in white writing on a white background, thinking they can fox a search engine. Others show pages with nothing else except keywords and content, with content written only for search engines.

Don't do it! It is not worth it. Some sites have been banned by search engines for this 'wrong side' business practice. Always weave your keywords into your page for your visitors' eyes only.

BLACKHAT MARKETING: Some sites use deceptive ways to drive traffic. This includes spam or cloaking within search engine result pages or routing users to pages that they didn't request. Don't go there!

Monitoring Keyword Performance

Keep up-to-date on how your keywords are performing by keeping a spreadsheet of your most important words in order of priority. I created a spreadsheet with our most relevant and popular keywords so I could track how fast we moved up the ladder. I had every intention of monitoring this on a month-to-month basis, but as you know there are so many other important things to juggle and before I knew it, we were Google's No 1. But not without lots of elbow grease! Try to avoid getting sidetracked and aim to do a quick search every month. Look for new trendy words, ones you may have missed and maybe even ditch the ones that don't work.

When people call us, we ask which search words they used to find us. If they are new words to us, we make a note of them and try them out.

Spreadsheet Items to Include
  - *Number of monthly searches*: you can get this from your Analytics
  - *Page to be optimised*: a link to the page
  - *Notes*: anything you want to remember in future
  - *On page SEO*: how you will use the words on your page
  - *Off page SEO*: list all possible link building sites

We will go through the various elements listed on this spreadsheet over the next few days.

Summary

Keywords are taking over our lives. We breathe, live, eat, sleep and even dream them. Without strategic keyword placement, your site will not only be a mish-mash of gobbledy-gook to the search engines, it won't be found by your buyers – those people you need and love.

Everything you have learnt today is all part of your Keyword Strategy and, assuming you use these methods and handy ways to include your keywords, you will become successful at optimising your website. Don't panic when you think about how much there is to learn and don't worry your head off if you think your keywords are not working. Give them time while you get to grips with the new keyword-rich world you live in. As I mentioned in the introduction, you aren't expected to do this in a few days. Take your time to understand and absorb each step before moving on.

In Day 3 we will learn what to do with the keywords and where to inject them into your site, which will ensure the search engines find your branded website. Put your feet up, have a glass of Rioja – you deserve it after all the excellent work you've done today!

Day 3
Keyword Tools

Today you will learn:

- The best keywords to use
- How to understand the power of keywords
- How to find the most effective keywords
- Which essential avenues to use to build a keyword list
- How to find niche and long-tail keywords

Keyword Tools

We have now learnt all the important rules of keywords and how to use them to cinch the penthouse suite in Google. So the time has come to discover where to find the richest words.

Luckily for us, there are so many fab resources and tools on the market today to boost your first attempt. We're about to strike keyword gold with some I have listed below. Of course, after this point (like me and all true keyword freaks) you will always be on the lookout for more really cool keyword tools!

The importance of these tools can only be seen once you have used the tools mentioned today and unearthed a vast range of keywords to use. This is not to confuse or muddy your already defined keywords. Instead, it will show you how to pick and choose new and different keywords to beat your competitors. You should also quickly recognise the significance of niche and 'long-tail' keywords and their relevance to your different landing pages.

Start with the search engines as they have their own keyword data. Type your most common keywords into Google and see what results come back. This demonstrates just how many searches were made in the past month (top right corner). You can also find keyword variations and start making a list of potentially promising words to use.

> *"Google Keyword Tool is a good, free device. Use Wordtracker for long tail phrases."*
>
> Ross Jackson, Ross Jackson Consultancy

How long will it take you to get up the ladder? That really depends on the level of competition for your keywords. Some experts believe it is relative to the number of competitive sites using your keywords. If you type your keywords into Google you will get an instant idea.

According to Ross, less than 1 million search results rendered is the fastest to crack; 1 million to 5 million is also relatively easy. While 5 to 10 million is difficult to achieve, more than 10 million requires lots of effort to rank high in search results.

Ross Jackson's Top Tool Tip

Use the Webmaster Tools provided by Google, Bing and Yahoo!

So if you look at a global Google search for 'Home Based Jobs', you will see that at the time of this book going to print there are more than 24 million results for 'Home Based Jobs' in the world! So a lot of effort was required for Remote Employment to achieve the number one position.

Of course at the time, I didn't think about this or even realise the enormity of the task, I simply did what I had to do. Don't let this faze you. Do what *you* have to do to achieve an excellent rank. Also note that we have a variety bucket of keywords and they all bring up different search result numbers. This may be the same in your case as well.

Pros

- ✓ Drive your keywords up the search engines
- ✓ Understand your visitor trends
- ✓ Conduct market research
- ✓ Generate new product ideas
- ✓ Write great content copy
- ✓ Press releases sprinkled with keywords
- ✓ Pay Per Click or other advert campaigns
- ✓ Monitor the size of your potential market

Cons

- ✗ Watch the costs
- ✗ Can be daunting with so many keyword results
- ✗ Consider a quick payment option, then decide if you need more
- ✗ Don't get hung up on KEI (Keyword Effectiveness Index) – more on this in a mo

Google's Keyword Tool

Google's Keyword Tool gives you the chance to include a website and a few keywords, which then searches the site and pops up with a whole new list of keywords to try.

Step-by-step:

1. Go to www.google.com/sktool.

2. Type in the website and some keywords.

3. Instant results with lots of keywords to play with.

The following image explains how to include a web address and a keyword example. Try each different keyword that is in your list and see what Google finds.

The example above shows you to what extent you can take your keyword research.

Google also offers you the chance to try a new tool that will generate ideas that are matched to your website, and based on Google search queries: www.google.com/sktool and adwords.google.co.uk/select/KeywordToolExternal

Wordtracker

Wordtracker (www.wordtracker.com) is another form of brainstorming. It's like an online brain that uses lateral thinking to spit out a hoard of possible words and synonyms. This clever system also takes keyword analysis one step further by suggesting related and specific terms and phrases, as well as niche words. Nifty, hey?

Well, I'm not done yet. Wait until you hear that you can even compare the number of keyword searches to the number of competing pages in all the different search engines. And you get to decide a competitive score for the keywords you've now collected. The competition count is based on data from the web, rather than search engines, although the Google Count can be a loose indication of competition, particularly with long-tail keywords.

It can be a minefield! So take it easy and don't get swamped with all the word combinations. It is a paid service that offers one day or one month options to new members and free trials.

Wordtracker also allows you to save projects and do tons of fancy exercises, including the following:

- Make an easy and quick start with the Wordtracker Keywords Tool to start searching for keywords
- Evaluate the competition and choose your keywords
- Filter and save your search results
- Find related keywords
- Quick 'search and save'
- Export your keywords – ideally to Excel for easy analysis
- Manage lists and projects
- Plan your SEO campaigns
- Plan Pay Per Click (PPC) campaigns

There is so much you can do and I won't spoil your fun and take you through each step, but I will point out a few interesting things I found. The quickest way to get started is to hit the button on your dashboard marked 'Start your keyword research'. For the purpose of this section, I tried some new keywords aimed to help me promote my books.

Use Territories

The following screenshot displays which button to click to change from the US to UK searches. Use this to further define your keyword results. You may also find niche keywords this way.

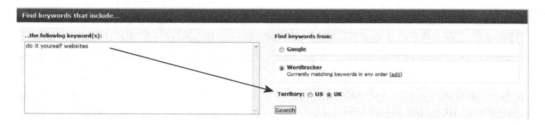

It's worth mentioning at this point that one keyword phrase can bring up different results from the UK and the US. The phrase 'make your own website' returned less results and keywords in the UK compared to the high volume returned from the US. The screenshot below shows how you can search Google data from a number of English speaking territories.

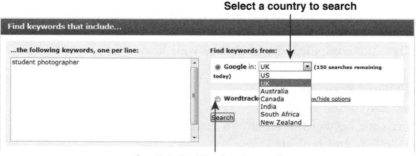

This country search only shows the Google interface, so be sure to search both US and UK data with Wordtracker as well by clicking their radio buttons.

Wordtracker will have updated their software between the time these screenshots were taken and this book goes to print. Online software tools are always subject to development so there may be some differences in what you see when you log in.

Additional Metrics

The metrics come down with the keywords and search counts in the first pass. You'll see the 'Get Google Count' button at the top of the list to the left-hand side. The following screenshot details how you can download additional metrics – follow the image and steps below:

1. See how many pages show this keyword result.

2. 'Searches' gives you the number of searches for that particular keyword.

3. 'Google Count': additional metrics give you the Google count, which is the number of pages Google has indexed for each keyword.

4. When you download the data, pick all columns as this info could come in handy in future.

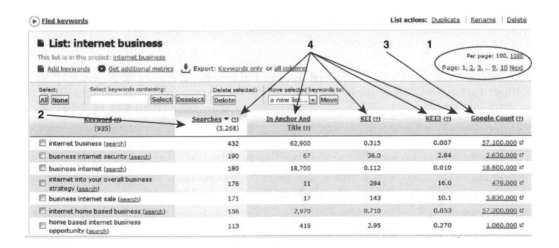

Wordtracker offers a 7-day trial. Or, if you have the budget, try a monthly or annual subscription and then you can take your sweet time. Whichever you choose, Wordtracker is well worth a visit.

Keyword (?) (10)	KEI (?)	KEI3 (?)
home based internet business opportunity (search)	2.95	0.270
home internet based business opportunity (search)	0.103	0.049
internet based home business opportunity uk (search)	0.195	1.00
based business home internet opportunity (search)	0.002	0.011
internet opportunity passive income home based business uk (search)	–	–
advertising based business free home internet opportunity (search)	0.222	1.00
based business home internet legitimate opportunity (search)	0.002	0.048
internet income home based business opportunity ma (search)	–	–
based business business home internet opportunity (search)	0.001	0.015
online based business home internet opportunity (search)	0.014	0.333

KEI

Wordtracker takes keyword analysis to the next level with their Keyword Effectiveness Index (KEI) metrics, which will help you spot niches with high popularity and low competition, as seen in the previous screenshot.

You need to find words that have a high search rating with not too many competitors using those words.

The KEI compares the number of times a keyword has been searched and found on competitors' pages that contain the exact keyword phrase. So the KEI figure will go up when the keyword's popularity increases and will go down when there is more competition for a keyword.

KEI3 combines a keyword's popularity (the number of searches) with its level of competition (text in your competitors' web pages) to help you find the keywords with the most potential. Consider both KEIs' suggested keywords and choose those that are most suitable for your website. You'll find more detailed notes on the metrics at: www.wordtracker.com/support/numbers.

Wordtracker recommend that their users view all the figures as relative values – it used to be possible to say that a KEI of X or Y was 'good', and Z was 'bad', but given the amount of optimised content on the web, and the different market sizes of each niche, it's better to look at the relationships of the keywords inside a niche rather than hunt for a 'magic number'. This is where the 'Related Keywords Tool' can prove invaluable in terms of building lists based on related keywords. This webinar recording shows you the details: www.wordtracker.com/academy/wordtracker-webinars.

Have a good play around to find the best niche words but, as I said before, don't get hung up on this. You might find it useful, as I did, to download the data from Wordtracker into an Excel sheet, so that you can then filter and sort the keywords by KEI.

Keyword Spy

While writing this book, I found another resource that may help your keyword quest – Keyword Spy (www.keywordspy.co.uk) also offers a free trial. You can do the following on Keyword Spy:

Domain Search: This search allows you to enter the domain name of the site you want to analyse.

The Keyword Search: This will let you enter terms and key phrases in the search bar, such as 'send flowers', 'business awards', 'keyword software,' and even a single broad term like 'chocolate'.

The Ad Copy Search: Enter any text or content included in an advert's copy, whether that is in the ad copy headline or in the description line.

The Destination URL Search: This search allows you to enter the destination URL of the site that you want to analyse. The destination URL is the address where a searcher is taken when an advertisement copy in search engines is clicked. Please take note that the destination URL differs from the display URL which appears at the bottom of advertisement copies.

Traffic Travis

Traffic Travis (www.traffictravis.com) is a one-stop-shop piece of kit. The all-in-one nub gives you access to fetch and find keywords, keyword suggestions, which is useful for both PPC and SEO campaigns.

The search count displays a number of daily searches for specific keywords in Google, Yahoo and MSN. It is ideally placed to find popular keywords in your niche or dig up long-tail search terms that are easy to rank for.

Next you get to filter, sort and save keywords to make sense of the otherwise huge lists you can easily accumulate during your keyword research. Try using Traffic Travis to group your keywords into topics or themes and don't forget to make the best use of this for defining Adgroups (coming up soon) for PPC or website landing page optimisation.

Traffic Travis also shows you how you rank and where your site appears in the search engine results for every word in your keyword list. Traffic Travis hunts through Google, Yahoo, MSN, Altavista and Ask to show you exactly where you stand.

Their competitor analysis monitors your competitors' movements in the search engines and remembers data from previous searches, so you can see whether a website is moving up or down the search engines over time. They have reports you can view daily, weekly, or monthly, which plot changes in your rankings. These create graphs to display the data visually. Remember to use this for showing off your Key Performance Indicators (KPIs).

Page Analysis
Page title, Pagerank, Alexa rank, Meta tags, heading tags and keyword density. All the nitty gritty 'on-page' factors of your website are laid bare with the click of a button. Traffic Travis throws in an on-page optimisation score to see how your page stacks up for a particular keyword. Traffic Travis gives you a rating based on factors that are known to boost your search rankings, including Meta tags, headings, page length, page content and more.

PPC Analyser

The larger your keyword sample list, the better your insight into your PPC market. Traffic Travis uses these words to find competitors, to see how strong your competitors are, and to spot profitable search terms that you might otherwise miss.

With Traffic Travis you can analyse your competitors' campaigns and find sites that are advertising with your keywords. And it shows your biggest competition, as well as showing you how their ads are performing over time. You can preview their ad right inside Traffic Travis. Talk about snooping!

Heavy competition means that there's money to be made. This software shows you the keywords that are heavily advertised, as well as pointing out keywords which experience a high turnover in advertisers, thus giving you the 'danger zones'.

Spy Fu

SpyFu (www.spyfu.com) believe their membership allows you to crack the codes of thousands of online companies that hold the time-tested optimisation secrets. Having full access to SpyFu reveals your competitors' trail of actions that paid off for them, their exact ad copy that drives leads and an over-their-shoulder peek at blueprints of their most-guarded online advertising plans.

Summary

As much as keywords are the most essential part to ensuring that your site will be visible and indexed on search engines, you should now have a good grasp about how to use them, where to use them and why you need them in your lives and on your sites. Hopefully, you are now more familiar with the main keyword tools too, and have an idea of which ones would be suitable to use in your keyword research. Spend some time getting a grip on those 'long-tails' as they can make all the difference in getting your site up the Google ladder. Make sure you don't fall into any of the keyword traps mentioned today and, above all, find some juicy places to use the delicious new words you have found.

While it can be pretty frightening seeing how keywords affect every aspect of your website's performance, it is also hugely exciting to know that if you work at finding the most effective relevant and specific keywords – especially niche and long-tails – for your content, your site will be found by potential clients and customers. Go through your keyword strategy again at the end of the book and decide where you will use your keywords and explore new places to use rich keywords. Don't be daunted by this complex world because we are about to break it down into smaller bite-sized chunks when we discuss SEO in Day 4. Your keywords will hit 'pay dirt' and help you to strike oil . . . or in this case 'Google Oil'.

Day 4
SEO

Today you'll learn:

- ■ How to ensure your website is optimised
- ■ To understand the difference between on page and off page optimisation
- ■ Where to implement keyword-rich content
- ■ How to perfect your page layout for best search engine performance
- ■ What metadata is and how to use it effectively

Have you Googled yourself or your site before? Try it and see what happens. If your site is already up and running you MUST Google it. Let's face it, when most people talk about searching they use the phrase, 'Have you Googled XXX?'

I repeat – your site MUST be Google-friendly. But of course, you know the name of your website and so you have Googled your company site. What about all those surfers who don't know you or your website name?

Today we will learn about optimising your site to get found by Google, MSN (Bing), Yahoo and the other top search engines. If the search engines don't know your site, neither will anyone else. You can't just sit back and wait for them to find you.

Great content and optimisation on your site will ensure long-term organic links and have the most impact on search results.

According to SEOmoz the top seven ranking factors are:

- 24% trust/authority of the host domain
- 22% link popularity of the specific page
- 20% anchor text of external links
- 15% on-page keyword usage
- 7% traffic and click-through data
- 6% social graph metrics
- 5% registration and hosting data

Read the full article to keep on your toes at SEOmoz: http://www.seomoz.org/article/search-ranking-factors

Search Engine Optimisation

What is SEO? It's one of those phrases that goes straight over people's heads and you can see their eyes glaze over as they try to digest its meaning. Essentially, it is the process of improving the ranking of a website within the search engine results. There are lots of different ways to get your website optimised so that the search engines will find you.

Go into SEO knowing that you're in for the long haul – and then some! Search engine optimisation is an evolving industry, and the search engines' robots, crawlers and spiders change their rules regularly so this is not a job for the faint-hearted. Be prepared to roll up your sleeves, get down and work your butt off to learn as much as you can to keep your website ranked high. You can't afford to 'ooze' tons of elbow grease and then sit back with your feet up. The fall from grace will be more painful than fighting the traffic to get to the front row.

SEO Basics

Don't be left standing at the starting gate while all the SEO horses gallop to win the Google, Yahoo and Bing race. Instead, teach yourself all you need to know about optimisation and how it works. This way you won't be left behind. However, if you end up deciding to get your developer or an SEO agency to do it for you, you will at least be in a position to know exactly what they should be doing for the money you pay them.

Some basic SEO techniques are listed below.

On Page Optimisation
- Correctly formatted metadata
- Keyword-rich content correctly placed on the page
- Targeted landing pages for relevant and specific keywords
- Site accessibility – don't hide content behind logins

On Page Optimisation deals with all the content on your page and how you use this to optimise the keywords for that particular page. Do remember that each page needs its own optimisation.

Off Page Optimisation
- Relevant inbound and outbound links

Off Page Optimisation is all about building links back to that particular page or to your home page. This is done via swapping links with other relevant sites that Google considers to be trustworthy.

All of this will give your website a higher ranking in the search engine organic results pages.

On Page Optimisation

There are certain steps to ensure each and every page on your site is properly optimised. We'll start with metadata.

Meta What?

Metadata is data about data, like a website index. Pimp My Site's table of contents is a meta-index to describe the book's details, such as the chapters, text and images. Therefore your site's page metadata is telling Google what your site contains, such as the page title, description, alt tags and keywords of each page. Metadata is added to 'Page Source'. In most cases, you can insert this yourself via your admin. Google 'reads' your pages through HTML code and MATCHES your page content to give a browser relevant search results.

I know this sounds scary, but you'll soon realise it's nothing to fear. You may not realise it, but you view Meta tags every time you see search results in Google and other search engines. The following screenshot shows the three essential metadata found in search results:

1. *Meta Title*: title tags

2. *Meta Description*: keyword-rich content description tags

3. *Meta Keywords*: keywords or phrases relevant to the page [shown above in bold]

Search engines use this Meta tag coding to find your site. Notice that the words 'business networking' are bolder. One of the ways Google found this page is when I typed in 'business networking'. Using primary keywords like this in your description, page title and keywords is vital in order to climb up the Google Ladder. You can visualise how your metadata will show in the search engines, so let's understand more about these meta kings.

We Three Kings of SEO

In the next few sections we'll explore the different metadata and their significance to your On Page SEO and learn how to implement them into your site.

Every page on your site MUST have these three kings specially selected and targeted from your list of keywords, but also choose them with specific relevance to your page. Some experts suggest that meta keywords are no longer used by search engines, but since no one really knows the exact methods used by Google and other search engines, it would be good practice to mix the three kings into your on page optimisation.

Meta Title

Keywords describing your page title are imperative. Some experts suggest this is the most important metadata for ranking, while others say it is the only metadata used in ranking today. It is the first piece of information about your website that someone sees in the search results. The title tag should be unique to each page, and should consist of your primary keywords, as close to the start of the tag as possible.

Meta Description

The meta description is a brief keyword-rich sentence or two about your page and confirms the phrase used in your meta title. It gives potential visitors a quick snapshot to see if the website is the right one. People will often read the description tag shown in the results page and if it's not what they're looking for, they won't bother clicking through to the site. So you must ensure your description is a synopsis of the page and, by being relevant and specific, you will receive targeted customers. Feature your 25 most powerful words to maximise those eyeballs scanning through search results and they will encourage people to click the link.

> ### Ross Jackson on Description Tags
>
> "It's a good idea to make this text both relevant to the search phrase you're targeting, and compelling for a potential site visitor, to encourage them to click your listing."

Take a look at the following screenshots. The first shows the meta title (1) and the meta description (2).

You'll notice that in the first screenshot, none of the keywords in the meta description are shown in bold. Why? This is because I typed the name of the company 'babyworld' instead of any actual keywords.

In this second screenshot, I used 'pregnancy' as keywords and found babyworld's search result. You can see here in bold that their keywords are embedded into their description.

Meta Keywords

These are the primary and secondary keywords that will be featured on a particular page. They emphasize the key message, to the search engines, about the page content's relevancy and specifics.

The following screenshot features the keywords I searched for in bold: 'business awards'. This shows the keyword phrase 'Business Awards' has been featured in three instances in one meta description.

This shows the effectiveness of featuring keywords within the webpage. So the correct use of keywords within the actual content on your page is just as important as the three meta kings.

I heard a penny drop! Is it all starting to fall into place now?

Understanding Meta

If the meta title, meta description and meta keywords are the three kings, then 'relevancy' is the queen. It is no good having spent time poring over the title, description and keywords only to plonk any old article onto the page. You must do your research before you start creating your page and understand these three main areas of Title, Description and Keywords.

My Top Tip

Build extra competitive advantage with the use of header tags, which are the first words that appear on your page. They are usually highlighted in a 'Heading 1' or 'H1' tag, as shown in this screenshot.

H1 Tag

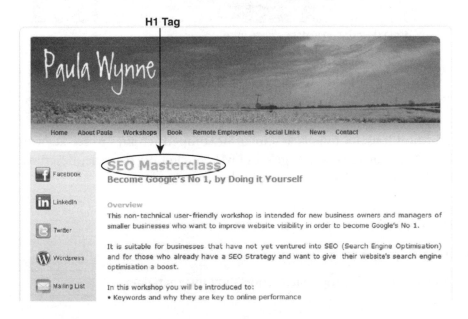

The following screenshot clearly demonstrates how the meta description on this babyworld page, found through the keyword 'pregnancy', matches the page introduction.

For example, some of babyworld's main words are pregnancy, baby, parenting and birth, but these words are not used on all the pages. Notice pregnancy is bold within the insert. The keywords are specific to the topic on the page.

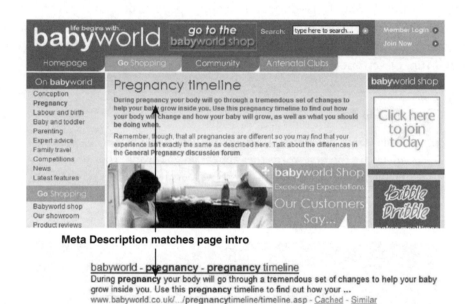

You might find it useful to look at similar or competitive sites to see keywords they have used. You can view any page's HTML, including the title, description and keywords by going to the page source in Internet Explorer:

1. Click on 'page'.

2. Then 'view page source'.

3. Window opens with the source code showing metadata.

For Firefox: click the down arrow in the orange Firefox button in the top left corner > Web Developer > Page Source.

Inserting Metadata

Most CMS systems have now integrated metadata into the admin sections, but do check with your hosted solution, pay monthly site or bespoke developer to ensure this is the case. You need it! Who has the budget to ask a developer to do this each time you add a page?

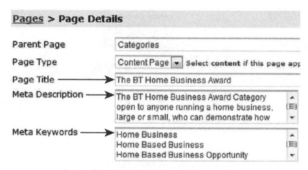

Inserting Metadata in admin section

This following screenshot above explains how you can easily add metadata to your website's admin section. The next screenshot shows you six areas to ensure you have metadata inserted:

1. URL

2. Breadcrumb (if you have this available)

3. Page Title

4. Meta Description

5. Keywords

6. Alt Tags

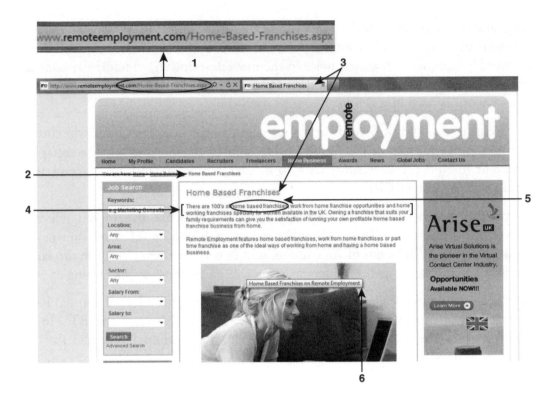

BREADCRUMBS:
A breadcrumb trail is a navigation aid that gives visitors a way to keep track of their locations within a busy site

Don't worry if all this is befuddling your brain, it should all start to make sense. I've been there, so I know how confusing it is, so applaud yourself for sticking it out so far! Now, let's tuck in and find out how to make all this come together.

Crucial On Page Targets

There are certain steps you must take to ensure each and every page on your site is properly optimised. Ensure that your primary keywords feature in the first paragraph like a grand statement, only do it in a subtle and intelligent way, weaving the words into your copy. Take another look at the previous babyworld screenshot to see how the word 'pregnancy' is featured twice in the meta description, which is the same as babyworld's page introduction, for their Pregnancy Timeline page. Also note that this keyword is used in a different context each time.

Be careful not to stuff keywords into your pages as the search engines will cotton on to you, and your readers will find it hard to follow bulky and cluttered paragraphs. First and foremost, your visitors have to be able to understand and appreciate a useful, well-written article.

To get the search engines winking at your pages, also use five to ten relevant keywords as linking text. These can either be internal links to other relevant pages within your site or links out of your site to linking partner sites. Don't use the same words again and again as the spiders may see this as 'stuffing' or 'spamming'.

Keyword-rich news releases and articles that provide valuable relevant content have an excellent chance of being found. Note that Google delivered The BT Home Business Award on Remote Employment's news pages when I searched for the 'business awards' as seen in this screenshot.

BT Home Business Award
Enter the **Home Business Award** if you work from home running your own home based business.
www.remoteemployment.com › ... › News › Awards › Award Categories - Cached

Alt Tags

An alt tag refers to alternative text, which is mainly used by web browsers that only display text and not images. It is one of the important functions of the Disability Discrimination Legislation because visually impaired visitors can use a text viewer when browsing your site. There are arguments for and against alt tags as some experts suggest that they are no longer used by search engines, and therefore are not important.

Use Keyword Alt Tags on all images

Work from home as a Party Planning Agent

However, to make your web images accessible to everyone, ensure that every image is tagged with relevant keywords, in the following screenshot and the search engines will pick up your pages based on the alt tag. My belief is – the more places you can entice a spider to crawl across your site the better. This concept has certainly worked for me.

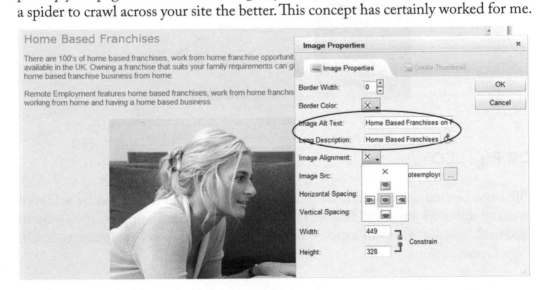

You saw earlier how the alt tag displays the alt text when your mouse hovers over an image. This alt tag text is inserted when you right click the image. Your WYSIWYG editor should also have an image-editor button in the top right corner. This is almost always a little icon of a mountain with a round orange or yellow sun. A window will open, similar to the one shown in this screenshot, where you will be able to insert the alt text and a longer description for accessibility.

Note that the previous image also shows you the image alignment, which allows you to choose whether you want the image left, right, top, bottom or centred. Varying your alignment makes a page more interesting and stylish.

My Top Tip

When inserting images, make sure your vertical spacing shows at least 7 to 10 points, viewed in the following screenshot, to allow a small gap between the image and the text so your content doesn't butt right up against the image, which makes your pages look amateurish. In saying that, even if you do this some browsers will format the alignment differently.

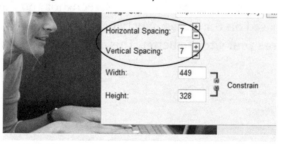

Off Page SEO

Off Page Optimisation is another phrase for link building, which can be achieved in many different ways. Building links with other sites and finding creative ways to link back to your site with articles, news and forum posts will enhance your On Page Optimisation.

Inbound and Outbound

One link comes into your site and another leaves your site, with inbound links gaining more credence than outbound links. The outbound link which goes off to another site relevant to yours, will obviously take your visitor away so do ensure that the link 'opens in a new window' so that your visitors can close that window and still find you in the background.

My Top Tip

The hyperlink editor in your CMS, which looks like a 'chain', will give you the option to open the link in a new window or existing window. For your own site use 'existing window' and for links to other sites always use 'new window'.

"Become an expert in your field through writing quality articles and posting them to directories."

Ross Jackson, Ross Jackson Consultancy

Inbound links are fuel to your site because search engines see this as a vote of confidence from the other website owner. Of course, links coming in bring the other site's traffic to your site so they will want a reciprocal link. This is the easiest and quickest way to build links. Newspaper coverage has given our sites great 'link juice' and if you get a story published they won't ask for a link in return.

How to Build Links

Start by searching all your competitors' sites and see which sites link to them. Then make a list of these sites, probably best done on another page in the SEO spreadsheet you created in Day 2, so you can contact them and request a link exchange. It is best to do this each time you find a good link exchange partner, as then it is a constant slow burn with links being built up over time. Add websites links to your spreadsheet with a contact name and email address and a date to help you keep control for future reference.

This means researching the best terms to use for relevancy and volume, starting to optimise your content and making sure you're asking for people to recommend you and link to you. Find a variety of good, valuable sites and request a link exchange with them. Don't even consider link farms as they could destroy all your hard work. You may have stumbled upon these sites before – they are just pages of links with no particular point or relevance to any topic.

There are also a number of sites that help you to compare your site with your competitors and gauge their link popularity against yours. Look at LinkPopularity (www.linkpopularity.com) and Submitexpress (www.submitexpress.com/link-popularity-check.html).

Find sites listed on your competitors' pages and approach them for a link, but do make sure they are relevant. We get approached every day for links which will have no benefit to our audience. You can also Google for sites that provide a paid-for service where they submit your links to their directory of sites. I decided not to go down this route as I didn't know who would be linking to us and didn't want to run the risk of devaluing our brand.

Don't be afraid to ask other sites for a link exchange, they can only say 'No'. If they do, move on and find more sites to swap links.

Directory Links

Setting up listings in web directories such as Yahoo! Directory and dmoz (www.dmoz.com) will improve your optimisation results. Some charge high fees and can take a long time to feature your entry but some directories to try are: BT Tradespace (www.bttradespace.com/freetojoin), FreeIndex (www.freeindex.co.uk) and Best of the Web (www.botw.org.uk).

According to Ross, there are several web directories that are known to be beneficial in terms of building up your link profile:

- dmoz: www.dmoz.org – free (can take 12 months+)
- Yahoo Directory: http://dir.yahoo.com – $299 annual fee
- Business.com: www.business.com – $299 annual fee
- Joeant: www.joeant.com – $40 one-off fee
- GoGuides.Org: www.goguides.org – $70 one-off fee

As I mentioned earlier, by asking for links from sites that are crawled regularly by the main search engines, you could be indexed much more quickly. You can also utilise Google's 'Free Directory Listing' and spend some time submitting your site. There are lists of directories that charge for submitting your site. You can also list your business the good old fashioned way with free local and sector directories. Here are some to try:

- Yell: www.yell.com
- Kyotee: www.kyotee.co.uk
- FreeIndex: www.freeindex.co.uk
- Parent pages: www.parentpages.co.uk
- UKClassifieds: www.ukclassifieds.co.uk
- Thomsonlocal.com: www.thomsonlocal.com
- ThciGroup: www.theigroup.co.uk
- StreetsLocal: www.streetslocal.co.uk

Beware of Link Farms

Link farms are sites that just have pages and pages of links and not much else. They are not the same as a web directory. Link farms are known to get webmasters into trouble so if anyone asks you to link to them and you see where your link will go, politely decline their offer of a link exchange. Not only will it harm your cyber relations with Google, but it will also devalue your brand. Even if you are desperate for links, don't use this link building method, as it's not worth it.

Google's Page Rank

Not to be confused with search rank, Page Rank is the score of importance that Google awards to websites. The following screenshot details where you can find the Page Rank button and, when you click it, it shows you your website's page rank.

Page Rank

- Page Rank is Google's measure of the 'importance' of a page
- Calculated via quantity and quality of inbound links on a particular page
- The higher the score the better. Best = 10
- BBC ranked 9, CNN 8, Sky News 6 out of 10

By optimising our online PR, we doubled the impact of the publicity by driving traffic back to our site. It also proved to be a fantastic exercise for us to increase our Page Rank. We jumped from nowhere to a 4 Page Rank and quickly moved up in importance to a 5 Page Rank. I asked John Straw, from Influence Finder (www.influencefinder.com), if the internet is beyond Page Rank.

"It was originally the formula that was used to calculate page authority for Google's algorithm. Recent deep web research by Influence Finder and several influential SEO bloggers indicate a subtle change in Google's algorithm. They believe Google is starting to look at a very broad range of factors beyond the link structure that was characterised by Page Rank. Relevance is an important area, as is site performance, which is judged by page loading time." John suggests that traffic performance could be a factor as well. After all, the more traffic you get, the more popular you are. So he believes that you shouldn't completely discount Page Rank. Instead look for relevant, established and well-trafficked sites to exchange links.

See this screenshot which shows where to locate the Page Rank button on Google on Everyclick's site (www.everyclick.com):

Good SEO Guidelines

As a quick fire summary on this section, which can be extremely daunting, here are a few short, snappy guidelines. They are not hard and fast rules, but over time an optimiser gets to know this by instinct.

- Page Title – up to 70 characters
- Description – 10 to 25 words
- Body Text – 200 to 800 words, and keyword phrases should appear up to 4 times
- Keywords – add 5 to 50 words, include 1 to 15 keyword phrases, and use them up to 3 times. Some experts recommend that this is bypassed by Google
- Images – add keywords in image title
- Videos – add keywords in video name and title
- Sitemap – make sure Sitemap is in place

Summary

Today we identified that building traffic needs constant attention. Combining with on page optimisation, off page optimisation and link building will, in time, bring you excellent results. Ensure your website is optimised with keywords and keyword-rich content as well as keywords on your alt tags. And use metadata to your advantage!

Google will honour you with a high rank if its crawlers and spiders consider your content to be important. Frequent updates and new page additions are monitored and recorded by these secret chaps. By using the tricks you discovered today, you should be able to get your pages so well optimised that Google will find and index them and consider your landing pages important.

Today we also explored how to create links in many different ways, by building links with other sites or using creative ways to link back to your site with articles, news and forum posts.

Day 5
Marketing Tools

Today you will learn:

- ■ To find the most popular SEO resources
- ■ The why, when and how of Pay Per Click
- ■ How to use Google Adwords
- ■ Where to use display and banner advertising
- ■ How to track traffic with Google Analytics

In Day 4, we learnt that SEO is about ensuring your site will perform well in the 'natural' listings for a specific search query. Today, we embrace search marketing tools including Pay Per Click (PPC), Google Analytics and various other tools to check your site is properly optimised. Let's first take a look at the various SEO resources available that may help you to optimise your site.

SEO Resources

There are a variety of resources that may help with your online marketing campaigns. I'll outline a few important resources here, but you can also search for 'SEO tools', 'optimisation tools', 'optimisation resources', 'SEM tools' or 'SEM resources'.

SEO Workshops

Have a Google for a workshop, seminar or training workshop as the knowledge you gain can give you a quick injection to the ins and outs of SEO.

Sitemaps

A sitemap is a map, directory or 'family tree' of your website pages and their links. It is best to always have a sitemap but it's really important when your site is new as it invites the search engine to 'see' all the pages on your site.

A sitemap has two fundamental uses:

1. It helps visitors navigate through your site pages, especially if your site is large. Each page is 'hyperlinked' so the visitor finds the page title and then links directly to the content on that page. They may also spot a page on your sitemap they may not have found just by navigating your site.

2. It assists Google's web crawlers to access and index all your site pages. The sitemap shows the 'bot' or 'spider' your entire site's page links in one place, which could be several levels of navigation in sub menus. Dare I say . . . a spider's feast!

Ideally your site will feature both an HTML sitemap, for the links on your page, and an XML sitemap to be submitted to Google and other search engines.

The XML should be checked often, especially if you have lots of dynamic links, to ensure it has no error pages and to feature new updates. Most XML sitemaps are automatically generated and can be submitted to Google via your Webmaster Tools in your Google Analytics Account.

SEOMoz

SEOMoz offers paid memberships where you will have access to their exclusive tools, processes and information that corporate clients use to dominate the search engines. Take their free month's trial, find them at seomoz.org.

SEO Book

SEO Book.com is a leading SEO blog by Aaron Wall. Aaron offers marketing tips and search analysis. He also offers training programmes with hundreds of articles, advanced SEO tools, training videos, downloadable strategy guides, and other resources packed with practical tips to help you market your website, build viral buzz, capture top search engine rankings, improve website monetisation, and increase conversion rates. Take a peek at www.seobook.com.

Scribe SEO

Scribe can help you in three important steps:

1. Scribe shows you the language and words your 'searchers' will use before you begin to write your page content or as you are doing it. Once your content is created, Scribe reveals instantly, or in 'real time', any keyword phrases you might have missed.

2. Scribe analyses your content, and then suggests ways in which you can tweak it to encourage search engine visits based on SEO best practices.

3. Scribe's link building tools help you assemble back links from other sites, crosslink the content within your own site, and identify influential social media users who want to share your stuff.

Scribe will lend a hand when it comes to discovering the correct and most profitable keywords for your relevant and specific content, which in turn helps to achieve higher search rankings and increase traffic to your site. This is a subscription-based service for Scribe Web, which also offers integrated versions of Scribe for WordPress, Joomla, and Drupal. Check their videos at www.scribeseo.com/demo-video

SEO PowerSuite

Within the SEO PowerSuite lies a toolbox of treasures: Rank Tracker, Website Auditor, SEO SpyGlass and LinkAssistant. These regularly-updated tools are battle-tested by SEO experts and website owners, but no special prep or knowledge is needed to use them, as the software guides you through each task. They have a free version for Windows, Mac and Linux.

Rank Tracker

Rank Tracker enables you to learn everything you need to know about your SEO rank. It even shows you if your site has moved up or down in search results, how many times this keyword is being searched, how powerful a keyword is and it has a built-in keyword suggestion feature. Best of all . . . Rank Tracker automatically checks your website's positions in any search engines you need, for any keywords.

WebSiteAuditor

WebSite Auditor helps you to optimise your entire website across the board, smoke out all problems that hamper its performance and learn the exact steps to optimise each webpage for any keyword in any search engine. Cool or what?

SEO SpyGlass

SEO SpyGlass automatically finds all pages linking to the site you specify. Their technology can find over 100,000 links for a domain and verify their SEO value. So you get a rich list of SEO-effective links, with contact info of linking sites' owners so you can contact them to ask them to give a link to you as well.

LinkAssistant

LinkAssistant will look at websites from all angles, and rapidly chooses hundreds of relevant high-quality websites and their contact info. You can then send out piles of personal link requests to convince site owners to link to you.

HubSpot

HubSpot offers inbound marketing software that helps businesses get found in search engines, blogs and the blogosphere, and social media. Once these qualified visitors are on your website, HubSpot helps you convert more of them into leads and paying customers through landing pages, lead intelligence and marketing analytics. Read more at www.hubspot.com.

Website Grader

HubSpot invented Website Grader, which helps you to check how well your site is doing, once it is optimised. It generates a free report on traffic, SEO problems, and how popular it is in social media. All you have to do is enter your URL and click Generate Report.

Don't be disheartened if the score is low – keep checking and use Website Grader's comprehensive report to spot errors to correct and implement improvements. If you want to jump in now and grade your site and your digital marketing, go to http://websitegrader.com.

> **Anthony Quigley on Search Marketing**
>
> Consumer search patterns are changing.
>
> This has to be delivered by you as the advertiser.
>
> Searchers don't like going to a site that doesn't deliver exact search terms, it frustrates them and they bounce off to another site.

Pay Per Click

PPC stands for Pay Per Click, which is an online advertising model whereby an advertiser will only pay for an advertisement when a user clicks on their ad. Whether this advert appears a thousand times or just once, the cost depends only on the number of times the advert is clicked through. Pay Per Click advertises your site, products or services in the 'Sponsored Links' or 'Paid Listings' of search engine results.

The amount that an advertiser stipulates as their maximum cost per click is not always the amount that is paid – the Google AdWords Discounter intelligently monitors the competition for each keyword and automatically reduces the actual cost per click to the lowest possible price per position on the page.

> *"PPC is the most controllable and measurable form of advertising ever devised."*
>
> Ross Jackson, Ross Jackson Consultancy

PPC advertising is said to be one of the greatest and most cost-effective ways to bring new visitors to your site. Advertisers spend billions in digital advertising. As a result, SEM is now the fastest growing form of advertising and, because of the complexities, many companies rely on agencies to manage their search marketing. The next few sections will guide you through the minefield in simple to understand explanations so that you can teach yourself how to market your online business through SEM.

The largest SEM providers are:

Pay Per Click

- CPC: cost per click – a set price paid each time a visitor clicks on an advert
- CPA: cost per acquisition is an agreed price for an 'acquisition' on your site, can be used for leads or ads
- CPM: cost per thousand is a set price per thousand ad impressions.

Anthony suggests that this is most common, but watch out as rates can soar for highly-targeted sites

SEARCH ENGINE MARKETING: Search engine marketing (SEM) is the combination of search engine optimisation (SEO) and Pay Per Click (PPC) advertising.

- Google Adwords
- YAHOO! Search Marketing
- Microsoft Adcentre

While Google is the dominant AdWords-serving search engine there are alternative servers. Yahoo (takes around 10%) and Bing (formerly MSN, takes 5%) are Google's main competitors, though neither have a particularly large market share in the UK. Keyword bidding is usually cheaper on these platforms because there is less competition from marketers on Yahoo and MSN.

Both Yahoo and Bing currently offer similar desktop editing tools and online management software to that produced by Google although there are subtle

 KEYWORD BIDDING: In Adwords, keyword bidding gives you the ability to set a different maximum Cost Per Click amount per keyword, rather than simply for the whole Ad Group. This enables you to target different keywords with different CPC amounts, while still showing the same ad copy. It is useful for targeting better-performing keywords with higher bids.

nuances among each of these programs. Bing is good for demographic targeting, as it utilises MSN Messenger data. The downside is that it doesn't have anything like the traffic of Google, but can still be expensive per click.

"Get PPC right and you can really excel. You advertise directly to that one person who types in your exact words."

Ian Dodson, Digital Marketing Institute

Pros

✓ Quick and easy to set up
✓ Instant 'paid' traffic while building organic SEO
✓ Target specific audience
✓ Test variations of your landing pages in order to improve conversion rates
✓ Measurable, controllable and effective

✓ Switch it on and off as you require, manage your budget. You can easily control your spending by capping your daily budget and by bidding on as many or as few keywords as necessary

✓ Best way to control the quality of traffic coming into your site – a user has to search for a keyword relevant to your ad campaign in order to see your ad

✓ With PPC you can also control which page of your website the user lands on. If you have particular content you wish to promote, such as a special offer or a new product, you can set up ads to land users directly onto that page.

Cons

✗ Could be costly if managed incorrectly

✗ PPC can be an expensive market to compete in as some keywords are much more expensive than others. Bidding on 'no-win no-fee solicitors', 'laser eye surgery' and 'car insurance', for example, can cost up to and over £10 a click.

✗ May need lots of tests before finding ads that work

✗ Daunting for the inexperienced user.

Good PPC management demands constant campaign monitoring because the search is user driven and search auctions are dynamic. Success depends upon users searching for your product or service and for you to be bidding at the right level for the most relevant keywords. If there is no search for your keywords then there is little point in running PPC campaigns.

If a user searches for 'car insurance' there would be next to no quality traffic for an ad that offers home and contents insurance even though the user has specified insurance in the search query. Similarly, an advertiser of fine wines will struggle to serve ads when users search for 'luxury yachts' despite the fact that both products share a common upmarket audience.

Google Adwords

Google AdWords allows an individual or business to promote themselves, their products and services with Pay Per Click (PPC) and site targeting services for both text and content media advertisements.

Once again you need to put yourself in a visitor's shoes and think like a buyer who wants your product or service. In a sense, you need to act as if you are searching for your own offering. Use the same thought process you obtained during your keyword research in Day 2 to consider who your 'customers' persona' is and what your site can do for them. It's also vitally important to establish what will make your advert stand out from your competitors. And don't forget to piggyback on their research by checking out their PPC campaigns.

My Top Tip

If you already have a Google account, you can simply add the Adwords link to your account settings: http://adwords.google.co.uk

Ad Scheduling

Ad scheduling allows AdWords users to specify the hours or days of the week when they want their ads to appear. This is best utilised by creating daily and hourly reports to find out when your ads are receiving the most valuable traffic (highest conversion rates, lowest cost per lead, etc.) and then timing your ads to coincide with these hotspots.

My Top Tip

Ad scheduling defaults to the account time zone, so if you are running it for ads abroad, check that you have accounted for the time difference.

Working in Regions and Geo Specific

The location and geo targeting tools on AdWords allow advertisers to specify where their ads appear from countries and territories all the way down to IP addresses within a 1km radius of a specific postcode. You can apply these settings at ad group level, allowing maximum flexibility over the exact regions where you wish your ads to be shown. AdWords will also allow you to custom build your own location targeting using the custom shape tool. This allows you to build your own specific target zone and therefore avoid any unwanted traffic sources such as nearby cities or towns that would otherwise fall under the target radius.

Useful Google Adwords Definitions

Below is a list of the terms you will discover when you start working with Adwords and PPC campaigns:

1. *Ad Rank:* Determines an advert's ranking on Google's search results pages. The maximum amount you're prepared to pay per click (CPC) Actual 'Click Through Rate' (CTR) % your ad is receiving = your Ad Rank.

2. *Ad Rank Score:* The position on the page where your advert is shown. The maximum cost per click an advertiser is willing to pay (Bid) × Quality Score of the ads used (QS) = Ad Rank Score.

3. *Quality Score:* How relevant your advert and its destination URL are for a particular search query. The core elements that make up the Quality Score are:
   (a) Click Through Rate
   (b) Relevancy of the keywords you're targeting
   (c) The quality of your landing page (destination URL)

Google defines this as 'relevant and original content, transparency and navigability'.

4. *Rates*: While 10% is excellent, it's also rare for a Click Through Rate – 3–5% is good and 1.5% is average.

Dan Fallon's Top Ad Group Tips

- Create multiple ad groups for large campaigns to make each ad more relevant to a particular service or product
- A max of 3 to 5 keywords per Ad Group
- Three actual ads per Ad Group. This allows for specific targeting of the keywords, so your copy matches what the searcher is looking for.

The recommended number of ads depends entirely on the size of the campaigns you are running (and the consequent number of ad groups) as well as your intended objectives. For example, if you want to promote hundreds of specific products or by various locations, then you should generate two generic ad texts so that the product or location can easily be substituted from ad group to ad group. If, on the other hand, you are promoting a special offer, then you should track and test multiple text ads to find the best performer and then remove the others.

Dan Fallon on Ad Groups

Ad groups are best used to split campaigns by specific products or services, allowing the advertiser to create ad text specific to a set of highly targeted and relevant keywords. Online retailers are a good example of how to use multiple ad groups because the more relevant the ad is to the search phrase the more likely the retailer is to make a sale.

If you were a sports retailer selling tennis rackets and shoes, then you might be tempted to put these two products in the same ad group with an advert for high-quality tennis kit. While this ad may still be relevant to a user searching for 'tennis rackets', a better strategy would be to separate tennis rackets and tennis shoes into their own ad groups with ad text specific to each of those products. In this case, the user would see an advert for high-quality tennis rackets rather than just an ad for tennis kit or tennis shoes and would be more likely to click through on the ad.

5. *Ad Campaign:* This is the overlying structure you give to the products or services you wish to advertise. You can define a set daily budget and the language and location targeting for all ads within a particular campaign. You should have multiple campaigns for different products or services to allow greater flexibility with your budgets and targeting.

6. *Rotating and Split Testing Ads:* Dan tells us that it often surprises people to learn how big an influence the actual ad has on conversion percentages and click through rates. This is often due to subtle variations in Quality Score, but equally important is the relevance of the ad to the eventual landing page. Split testing landing page performance for conversion percentages is a quick way of working out which pages of your site users prefer. Other good strategies include ensuring that keywords are in the ad text and rotating ads to test which ad text receives a higher click through rate.

For example, you have two identical ads, except for the headline. Once you have an ad that performs better (which you might define as having a higher CTR, if this is your goal), you keep the headline from that ad on both ads, and alter another element, such as description or links.

> *"Adwords is the best marketing tool because people come to you."*
> Anthony Quigley, WebKitchen

New Online Marketing Frontiers

Marketing on the web is different to marketing offline and requires a different approach. It is certainly good to follow others and copy their successes, but as you refine your ad campaigns don't be afraid to brave new frontiers with novel ideas.

Start by monitoring the success of everything you do, especially your 'click through' rates, to see what messages work best.

Use matches to improve search results along with split testing to recreate the best-performing ads across all your ad groups. The one that works the best is your 'control ad' and then you only need to implement slight changes. Your aim is to beat the 'control advert', but you will need to experiment to get used to how it works.

Use these match types to improve your advert targeting:

keyword = broad match
"keyword" = match exact phrase

[keyword] = match exact term only
- keyword = don't match this term

Work with three varying ads per Ad Group and start by tailoring ads with slight keyword changes. If you can see a particular keyword is attracting the most clicks in its Ad Group – spin it off into its own Ad Group to try and make it more effective.

Don't forget those niche keywords and long-tails from Day 2 to get better rates. Targeting your niche keywords and long-tail keywords will be more effective if you develop specific adverts for them, so your copy matches the terms your browser has searched.

As research suggests, people are more likely to click on all main words that are capitalised, try out some snappy catch phrases. And . . . test, test, test!

Dos
✓ Do limit the number of keywords per Ad Group
✓ Do split test adverts based on copy, display and destination URLs, CPC
✓ Do measure and test on an ongoing basis

Don'ts
✗ Don't set it and forget it
✗ Don't fall foul of Google's guidelines
✗ Don't give Google all the control – decide for yourself which advert is working best and optimise it accordingly

Dan Fallon's Top Dos

1. Separate products and services into different campaigns and ad groups.
2. Write ad text relevant to the keywords.
3. Land users on the most relevant webpage to the ad text.

> ### Dan Fallon's Top Don'ts
>
> 1. Don't broad match every keyword and use phrase or exact matches where practical.
> 2. Don't set a daily budget beyond your means.
> 3. Don't use the display network unless you have experience, it can get very expensive very quickly.

"The most important thing about digital marketing is testing your Adwords campaigns. If you don't test you'll never know what's working and how to improve."
Ross Jackson, Ross Jackson Consultancy

In this way, social media PPC allows advertisers to custom create ads targeting niche products at niche markets without worrying about receiving clicks from uninterested users.

Highly Targeted PPC

Due to the nature of social networking, you can zero in on your target audience by using specific demographic data found on sites such as LinkedIn and Facebook, which both offer their own version of a PPC service.

> ### Ross Jackson on PPC
>
> Start with the research you did with your keywords – this is the best route for PPC on other networks:
>
> 1. Keyword research
> 2. Match the keywords in the ad copy
> 3. Maximum 4 to 5 keywords per ad group
> 4. Measure and test
> 5. Test some more.

Facebook Ads

Facebook also offers Pay Per Click advertising. You can target your ad by location, gender, age, keyword, relationship status, job title, workplace, or college. As you select each targeting criteria, a nifty little box pops up on the side and displays the approximate number of users that your targeting encompasses. The numbers can be a little mind-blowing! Facebook recommends you bid for each click or you can pay per thousand impressions. The 'bid estimator' will show you the range of bids that are currently winning the auction among ads similar to yours.

Facebook has an ads guide at www.facebook.com/adsmarketing, but in the meantime, here are some Facebook terms you should familiarise yourself with.

Campaign: The title you've given your ad campaign.

Status: Your campaign can be active and running, paused or temporarily stopped, but able to be restarted or deleted.

Budget/day: The amount you've indicated you're willing to spend on that campaign per day. You'll never be charged more than this amount.

Clicks: The number of times users have clicked on the ads in this campaign.

Impr.: Impressions, or the number of times the ads in this campaign have been shown to users on the site.

CTR (%): The click-through rate for your campaign. This is calculated as the number of clicks received divided by the number of impressions.

Avg. CPC: The average cost per click for this campaign. This is calculated as the amount spent divided by the number of clicks received.

Spent: The total charges accrued by this campaign.

LinkedIn Ads

As with Facebook and Google, LinkedIn also provides a similar advertising service.

Adverts

The best way to start is to create multiple ads for each campaign, then you can decide which ads perform best. Don't forget to use action verbs in the headline and choose words that grab the attention of your target audience and clearly explain what you offer. Eye-catching headlines and promotional offers will get more attention and should describe the products or services offered.

Be sure to highlight your special offers, unique benefits, whitepapers, free trials or demos and, wherever possible, include an image with your ad that's relevant to what you offer.

You could also try an advert variation with a question in the headline to engage people showing clear benefits together with strong call-to-action phrases like 'Try Now', 'Download', 'Sign up', or 'Request a Quote'.

Targeting

Research which audience to target and narrow your target audience to people you know to be interested in what you offer. It goes without saying that you should create ads that will appeal to that particular audience. By doing this, your ad becomes more relevant and will receive more clicks. You can also target by Geography, Job Function and Industry.

Budgeting

It is vital to set an appropriate daily budget (maximum amount that you are willing to spend each day). You'll find that the Suggested Bid Range is an estimate of the current competing bids by other advertisers. The higher your bid within the range, the more likely it is for your ad to be shown and receive clicks.

Performance

While your click-through rate (CTR) is a good indicator of how your ad is performing, good ads have a CTR greater than 0.03%. If your CTR is lower than 0.03%, create and test several additional ad variations by following the suggestions for creating great ads listed above. You can significantly improve the click-though rate with small changes to your ads. The ads that perform best are relevant to the target audience and are written with clear, compelling words.

Some ads working better than others.

Campaign	Status	Daily Budget	Clicks	Impressions	Click Through Rate	Avg. Cost Per Click	Total Spent ▲
Drama Award	On Turn Off Hide	$10.00	8	51181	0.016%	$2.00	$16.00
Freelancer Award	On Turn Off Hide	$10.00	12	33083	0.036%	$2.00	$24.00
Internet Business Award	On Turn Off Hide	$10.00	4	6287	0.064%	$2.00	$8.00
Total for All Campaigns			24	90551	0.027%	$2.00	$48.00

I would suggest that you look at each of these key online advertising platforms, as well as the main search engines to gauge which is the best for your target audience. First and foremost you should consider the target audience of LinkedIn's platforms compared to yours along with each of the key online advertising platforms, including the main search engines. This should help you to gauge which is the best advertising medium for your target audience.

> **Dan Fallon on Facebook and LinkedIn PPC**
>
> Search PPC is user driven because a search query should generate ads relevant to their search. On Facebook and LinkedIn, this isn't possible; the only way to target users is by the demographics that they define for themselves.
>
> This isn't necessarily a bad thing, as target demographics can be defined by their age, location, gender but more importantly by their interests, employment history and 'likes'. For example, Facebook would attract a mainstream audience, primarily younger consumers (although it is drawing in new market segments daily). LinkedIn, on the other hand, concentrates on B2B (Business to Business) audiences and may be a better target for connecting with working professionals.

"

Dan Fallon's Guide to Setting up an Adwords Campaign

Tweak this template for your own site. Go over your keywords and follow these steps to ensure you get the most out of your Adwords groups and campaigns:

1. Set up an AdWords Account for www.yourdomain.com and download AdWords Editor.
2. Load your account in Editor and add a new CPC campaign. Set the campaign status to Paused and check that location and language targeting are set to UK and English (UK).
3. Create the first ad group for this campaign and set the search bid to £1.00 and leave all other bids at £0.00.
4. Consider the keywords people might use to make the ad appear, thinking about how these will be relevant to what your website will offer. Remember to consider the character limits: 25 characters per headline, 35 for each line of ad text and 35 for the display URL.
5. Click into the Ads tab: what do you want people to see when your ad appears? What are you offering? Is your ad text relevant to the keywords they searched for?
6. You're now ready to run an Adwords campaign, but first consider these remaining points:
   Have you got the right match type for your keywords? Use the broad match modifier.
   Have you included any negative keywords? What searches don't you want?
   Are you testing more than one ad text? Produce alternatives and test for performance.
7. Once you are satisfied with that ad group, start a new one.
8. You could also create a new campaign with multiple ad groups: for example, one for your own brand and a second **based on your competitor's brand**. This could give you more brand visibility and potentially steal clicks away from your competitors.
9. Remember to monitor and refine your campaigns.

"

Display Adverts

Like Adwords, display ads are designed to drive traffic to your site except that they use a visual image and the advert is linked to a landing page on your site.

Display ads are great for branding, and big brands can get a better impact from using them. Do remember, if you don't have an image or brand that is immediately recognised it is harder to get people to click through to your site. Display ads can be direct – you create the ad and then pay to advertise it on other sites – or they can be implemented through an ad server or affiliate merchant account. Ads placed at the bottom of a page are less intrusive, but most advertisers like to get their message across quickly at the top of the page, particularly in the top right corner. This is 'prime property' on a site.

> *"Target your display ads by lifestyle, demographic, geographic and audience behaviour."*
>
> Anthony Quigley, WebKitchen

Display ads are mostly in gif, jpeg, png or JavaScript formats. They come in a number of sizes, but the most common ones are:

- Leaderboard: 728×90
- Medium Rectangle: 300×250
- Wide Skyscraper: 160×600
- Small Rectangle: 180×150

My Banner Ads Top Tips

- Ensure they are quick to load on the page
- Add a quick call to action
- Key message must be prominent
- Don't try and fill the space, people won't read it
- Always, always insist on good quality graphics
- Link to the relevant landing page on your site
- Don't go overboard with animation and flash
- Use alt tags – if someone blocks the banner they will still be able to read your message

Check the Interactive Advertising Bureau (IAB) site's guidelines on display ads at www.iab.net.

Web Analysis

There are various software programs and online tools that give you the ability to analyse and measure your traffic. However, most experts consider Google to be the best, the most advanced and most up to date.

Google Analytics

Google Analytics is a tool to measure your traffic, KPIs (Key Performance Indicators), and overall website performance. The benefits include: overall site performance (see your KPIs in action), monitor the impact of page content, understand which marketing campaigns are working and which ones are not working. Consider measuring web visitors, conversion rates, and costs if you are using PPC and keywords.

You can track Adwords results in Google Analytics by linking your Adwords account to a Google Analytics account. The main benefit of this is that you can separate paid search results (from PPC) and non-paid search results, allowing you to compare performance and calculate a definable return on investment for your Adwords campaigns.

My Top Tracking Goal Tips

Decide on your objectives. This could be to increase sales, grow audience traffic or monitor new products or services. Identify the key things you need to measure, such as tracking a contact form or building a mailing list.

> **Ian Dodson on Google Analytics**
>
> Best free tool you'll get in the online space. There are hundreds of alternatives, but this is best for analysing traffic. The downside is that there is no 'human' support. Decide what info you need to analyse and Google will deliver.

Useful Google Analytics Terms

What do the metrics mean? Here is a list of the various terms you will find when using Google Analytics:

1. *Unique Visitor:* A person who has visited your website at least once (measured by their unique IP address), in a fixed time period, which can be per day, per week or per month. This term is used in web stats to count each visitor to your website once in the time frame of the analytics report. So for example, if they visit your site seven times a day they will only be counted as one unique visitor for that day or week or month. This stat is used to measure your site's true audience or 'reach'.

2. *Bounce Rate:* The percentage of visitors who bounce away to a different site, rather than continue on to your other pages. This happens when a new visitor only views a single page on your website and leaves without viewing any of your other pages. A high bounce rate generally indicates that site entrance pages aren't relevant to your visitors. They land, take a quick glance around, think, 'Mmm, not for me' and off they go again.

 My Top Tip

Think of it like someone sitting in front of the telly with the remote in hand, flicking between channels looking for something to watch. It they don't like the look of a programme, they're gone in seconds.

3. *Conversion:* Whether your visitor reaches a defined goal, which you have set up. This helps you to see how good your site is at turning traffic into goals, which can be as simple as signing up for an event or registering on the site or paying for an item. It gives you the ability to gauge how effectively your site is working. For example, you may want to track a sales process from your home page or landing page right through to a product purchase.

4. *Dwell Time:* The time the visitor spends on site. This stat is often highly regarded as it can show how long people actually browse through your valuable content. However, this may not be completely accurate as Google cannot see if someone has nipped off to make a cup of tea. The visitor may also have multiple tabs open and therefore their eyeballs are not always focused on your pages.

5. *Hit:* The number of hits from a site.

6. *New Visit:* A completely new visitor.

7. *Returning Visits:* A returning visitor who has been on the site before, but comes back for another session.

8. *Page Impression or Page View:* A page opened by a user. Ross refers to this as a 'measure of volume'.

With these metrics, you can find out a lot of useful information, such as the following:

Visitors – define your site demographics by looking at who visits your site:
　　1. The number of visitors over a period of time
　　2. How often they visit
　　3. New versus repeat visitors
　　4. The countries they come from

Traffic Sources – analyse which keywords are best and which sources in your DMS are bringing traffic to your site:
　　1. What drives traffic to the site
　　2. Which campaigns are working
　　3. Which search keywords are used

Content – test your On Page SEO with the most visited pages and make improvements to the least visited pages:
1. See which pages are attracting most traffic to the site
2. Are there any problem pages, such as those with a high bounce rate?

Conversions – create reports to see if you are driving leads and converting sales or enquires
1. See the conversion rate
2. See which pages drive sales or enquiries
3. Work out whether visitors drop out through key processes, such as Checkout, Registration or Contact pages

By tracking the various results – especially traffic, leads and sales – you will know which plan is working the best and it will enable you to enhance this part of your strategy.

My Top Tip

Experiment and test for best results.Click every link you find in your account to see what happens. Play with the graphs and reports. Go through each section's pages to gain a better understanding of this intelligent tool.

Key Points About Google Analytics
- *Set Up:* Go to http://www.google.co.uk/analytics to set up a Google Analytics account and profile.
- *Filters, Goals and Funnels:* Ross suggests that you filter out internal or in-house traffic so your own use is not counted. It will also enable you to map out successes and events as goals, such as which products are bestsellers. It certainly makes sense for larger companies with lots of employees accessing their site daily.
- *Add Code:* Add the basic code on your website to enable tracking.

- *Ecommerce and Events:* Tracking ecommerce revenue, and other key events (e.g. downloads, videos, flash usage).
- *Marketing Campaigns:* Monitor your PPC, emails, banners and social media campaigns through Google Analytics.

Summary

It is vitally important that you monitor your online marketing, your traffic, audience demographics, KPIs and overall web performance. Our experts all advise that Google Analytics is the best free tool to accomplish this.

The best way to learn Google Analytics is to experiment with it by having a good ol' play around. Click every link and button, and then carefully assess the results. When you measure the process you can optimise further activity based on the results.

If you're still confused with Pay Per Click advertising, consider finding a quick and easy course on PPC and Google Adwords. Otherwise browse through all the documents and resources that Google offer. You can also download their 'Google University' which has all Google's products in easy steps. Then download the free SEO resource tools and use them to check your on page optimisation.

Day 6
Online Marketing

Today you will learn:

- How to use bookmarking and social buttons
- The why, when and how of blogging
- How to use article marketing to drive traffic and back links
- Why you need to build a reputation as an industry expert and with eBooks

We've already discovered that there are a number of marketing tools available to increase traffic to your site. Today we'll meet share buttons and other social bookmarking options, as well as Article Marketing and eBooks, and how to use them to drive even more hits. Look out for Facebook's 'Like' icon (that little thumbs up sign you may have seen on web pages) coming up in Day 9.

SOCIAL BOOKMARKING: Easy ways to access, class, file, share and search links that are combined in a single site.

Bookmarking

You are probably familiar with the various social bookmarking buttons and how to use them. You may even share your favourite sites with your network of friends and colleagues. You will see a great little 'share' button on all the best sites and you should be using its functionality to connect your customers and prospects via email, IM (Instant Messaging), blogs and social networks, along with word-of-mouth referrals. While Digg, StumbleUpon and Delicious are the most popular, take a peek at the others.

When it comes to buttons, there are all sorts to choose from and you can simply Google 'share buttons' to see the raft of options. It's personal preference, but I like the 'Tell-a-Friend' button, which can be designed as a customised share button, along with a custom 'Tell-a-Friend' widget to brand all word-of-mouth referrals from Social Twist.

WIDGETS: A widget is a cool gadget that can be set up in various online platforms to create nifty tools to insert HTML code into your site.

Some Share buttons to try:

www.digg.com   www.delicious.com
www.stumbleupon.com   www.addthis.com
www.reddit.com   www.sharethis.com
www.propeller.com   www.socialtwist.com
www.mixx.com   www.socialfollow.com

Gigya – Making Your Site Social

While building and developing our new social networking site, iHubbub, a social network for the Home Working World, I wanted to find one standard option that would fit snugly into our lovely new site. This is when Gigya came to the rescue. Gigya is a fantastic social sharing platform that offers one API (Application Programming Interface), enabling you to

API: An application programming interface (or API) is a way for developers to access automated, updated and dynamic content and feed it into your site.

bring the power of social networks to your site and thus drive registrations, traffic and user engagement.

Gigya works by integrating your online business with the top social networks in one place, similar to the old 'one-stop-shop' where all your favourite shops were under one roof in a shopping mall.

The API allows community members to log in to your site using their existing social networks, which is believed to increase conversions by 100%. When a visitor clicks on a social media icon, Gigya asks them to authorise the access, just like with any other secure online application, and they start social sharing. The screenshot below shows how the Gigya solution prompts your visitor to share the results at relevant moments and feed them simultaneously to their social networks, which are dynamically published in their social stream.

Each 'share' is estimated to drive at least five new visits to your site. I have set this up for the most important interactive areas of our new site as well as for posting or adding content. So, when a member adds their 'user generated content', a window pops up and they are asked to share their content. You can also set their 'micro-blog' post message with a prefilled message. They can change this, of course, but it gives you the chance to sprinkle your keywords across your visitors' social platforms.

Gigya also gives you an activity feed plug-in to bring community activity to life, creating a more social and engaging experience from the start. The activity feed increases page views and time spent on your site, driving visitors deeper into your site via a real-time stream of user activity on any page. This kind of activity display creates instant personalisation and social context for your community.

Gigya also supplies a live chat plug-in for IM (Instant Messaging). Chat messages are syndicated directly into the visitor's social media content, driving referral traffic back to your site and, in so doing, creatiing an instant 'buzz' because the visitor can choose to view all conversations or just those of friends.

To round it all up, Gigya provides analytics reports about which users are sharing the most and driving the most referrals back to your site from their social sites. Phew! Pretty damn smart, don't you think? See all this in action at www.gigya.com, but do be aware this may be memory hungry and thus affect page load speeds so check with your developer.

Blogging

Essentially, blogging is a web log or journal of the blog owner's thoughts. It also allows for regularly posted content or articles. For the savvy digital marketer, a blog is a key marketing tool. Blogs allow you to engage in a conversation with your customers while improving your website's search engine rank.

The Benefits of Blogging

- Blogging increases SEO
- Some blogs are ranked before the owner's website if keywords are added to optimise the blog
- Blogging grows social news and networking sites
- Lots of widgets and gadgets available
- Interact with your audience – people can comment on your topic and you get to build online relationships

Dee Blick's Top Tip

Remember, if you are writing in your capacity as a business entrepreneur you must follow the business code – avoid expletives, ranting and excessive self-promotion. Think about what you can share that has real value. Your blog must entertain and inspire. It should be an extension of what 'You' stand for in the real world.

Remember in Day 5 when we learnt how search engines love to munch on new and changing content? Writing a blog is an ideal way to constantly add fresh keyworded content. A blog allows you to engage with your audience whilst increasing traffic to your site. If you have a B2B site and have to stick to corporate language then this is your chance to show some personality and, in doing so, you will get more links.

> *"Don't create a blog, create a blogging culture."*
>
> Andrew Seel, Qube Media

Use the opportunity to trial, test and knit different keywords into your text and see how they perform. The key aspect to blogging is to show your brand's personality and in a sense humanise it. Blogs feature a wide range of diary-type entries, from personal to corporate, across a huge assortment of subjects. Some are personal journals of the author's daily life, while others are meanderings of topics or ramblings on debateable issues.

Get into Blogging

In my previous book (*Create A Successful Website*), I discussed setting up a blog as a good way to get familiar with using the internet as a web 'owner' and getting online in a flash. Marketers and website promoters use blogging to create fresh content quickly to draw in search engine visitors.

> *"A business blog allows you to connect in a two-way dialogue with potential customers and keep them constantly engaged with your company."*
>
> Dee Blick, Marketing Gym

If you are starting out and not sure what you want to do, try setting up a free blog in Blogger or Word Press. This will give you experience working with a website, show you how to add pages and content, and how to implement widgets and gadgets into your site. Take a look at www.blogger.com and www.wordpress.com. Read more about best practice blogging at www.probloggerbook.com and www.problogger.net.

In the meantime, here are some common blog traits:

- Content listed in chronological order, newest on top
- Archives of older articles
- Place for people to leave comments

- A Blogroll, which is a list of related sites
- Feeds such as RSS or other files
- Wide variety of templates
- Side columns with all sorts of widgets and gadgets
- Capability to schedule blog posts to publish articles automatically on a certain date. This is handy if you do batch blogs when you have some time and then they are uploaded over a period of time

REALLY SIMPLE SYNDICATION (RSS): Really Simple Syndication is clever technology to allow you to subscribe to a website's content with a direct feed.

RSS READER: The application to monitor your selected feeds.

My Top Tip

Blogging should be a central part of your inbound marketing strategy. It produces fresh, targeted content and helps attract more inbound links, which improves your search engine rankings.

"Blogging is the best tool for SEO. Consider it as content – the more you have the more valuable Google sees it. It brings people in, but also brings Google in."
Ian Dodson, Digital Marketing Institute

Be a Brilliant Blogger

Given that the power to blog is available at your fingertips, not to mention the fact that you can set up your own blog for free, Dee Blick believes that by this stage in the book you should be itching to get started . . . and gives her suggestions for being a brilliant blogger. Before your fingers start clattering across the keyboard, stand back and take a moment or two to think about your blogging strategy. If you are blogging within a business context, it's your business name, carefully designed brand and your reputation that's on the line each time you publish a blog post. This applies whether you are blogging on your own site or you're responding to articles and blog posts online.

My Top Tip

Brand yourself as a blogger by always using the same image, either of yourself or the same Gravatar (your own icon).

Dee Blick's Guide to Blogging

A blog is meant to be an informal and informative communication.

1. Draw up a loose programme of blog topics.
   You can share a business experience; your thoughts on a great book, a client case study that you know will be helpful, insights on what it takes to be successful.
2. Stuck for inspiration?
   Start by studying the blogs of business people that you admire. You'll soon come up with a list of do's and don'ts.
3. Decide on the frequency of your blog posts.
   Ultimately, you want people to subscribe to your blog so get into the habit of expecting to read your blog. The secret lies in keeping it up week in, week out whether you are up to your eyes in work or not. Tough call!
4. How long should your blog be?
   It can be as little as 100 words – you may want to share an inspirational quote that you have read in a book. However, aim for around 300 to 350 words per blog post.
5. Don't court controversy.
   Remember, you are aiming to attract people to your blog within a business context. Save the controversy for your social conversations. Your blog is there for anyone and everyone to see.
6. Be your own harshest critic.
   Write your blog, leave it for a few hours or days and then revisit it with fresh eyes and a red pen. If you don't trust your editing skills consider using a freelance editor.

7. Promote your blog.
   Don't forget to tweet and 'micro blog' on your social networking sites as well as the sites where your target readers hang out. Promote it at networking events and include it on all printed communications.
8. Have a trial run.
   Before your blog posts go live, do a trial run with people whom you trust to give their honest opinion.
9. Invite feedback on your blog posts.
   Ask for feedback in the final line of each post. You have the option to publish comments unaltered or to edit them.
10. Build your online brand.
    Remember, the ultimate aim of your blog should be to assist in building your personal brand and your business brand online. You should aim to share freely with a good heart. Do so with style and panache and who knows where your blog may take you.

Blogging Resources

Try blogging feeds to get all your blog interests and topics in one nifty place (e.g. Technorati, Blog Pulse and Bloglines). Go to blog.grader.com and www.hubspot.com to measure your blog's marketing mojo.

Download a Business Blog Marketing Kit to learn how to implement a successful blog marketing strategy. Hubspot includes three how-to videos and an instructional eBook: hubspot.com/blogging-kit.

Consider becoming a guest blogger and spread your blogging messages. Try myblogguest.com and bloggerlinkup.com.

If you have Windows 7 or Vista, use Windows Live Writer to compose your blog posts. It allows you to add photos and links to your videos, and then publish straight to your blog. Live Writer can also be accessed offline.

Article Marketing

Steve Shaw, from Submit Your Article, defines Article Marketing as using the power of free reprint articles to effectively market your website.

As a website owner you can effectively build links, increase search engine ranking, drive traffic to your website, and establish yourself as an expert in your niche, all with a few quick and easy syndication tools. Get Steve's report at submityourarticle.com.

> *"Article Marketing is a niche within Digital Marketing. It is another way to get links."*
>
> Ian Dodson, Digital Marketing Institute

Pros
- ✓ Most article marketing sites are free
- ✓ Write what you know to express passion and energy
- ✓ Using a syndicated site creates a viral effect
- ✓ Feature the article on your site as well
- ✓ Can increase back links, traffic and page rank

Cons
- ✗ Can be time consuming to write and submit articles
- ✗ You need to be able to find ideas and write a decent article
- ✗ Some sites may charge
- ✗ Unauthorised modifications can occur
- ✗ Risk of losing control of the article if someone does not credit your site

My Top Tip

Use Google alerts to keep track of where your articles are published. This will help you keep an eye out for unauthorised modifications or incorrect/absent acknowledgement of your site.

Anatomy of a Great Article

Essentially, an article is taking your best content and turning it into an article. You will lay the article into the same format as your sticky content (good value content that brings visitors back to your site), breaking it down into paragraphs with headlines and sub headers. The written article must be interesting and should inspire the audience.

The article must include a catchy title and headline to give a brief introduction of your article topic. Always try to reach out to, motivate and inspire the reader with a clear benefit. At the end, summarise and wrap up with a key message and don't forget to credit yourself (the author) with a bio or resource box. Also use this space to mention your expertise and other articles. You can also upload any articles on iHubbub to increase your chances of back links as we have set up natural optimisation for all our members articles.

How the Viral Works

Each time someone reads your article they will see your resource box, which includes information about you and your business along with a link back to your website. So, every time the article is picked up for publication your name and a link back to your website are published as well. In this way you build links and increased exposure for your website.

My Top Tip

Have several one-liners in your resource toolbox and use them for different promotions or offers.

Syndicate Articles

As we know, Google likes fresh updates and constant new links so this system is an ideal way to spread your message across the net with scheduled feeds.

Distribution Channels

EzineArticles.com: www.ezinearticles.com

GoArticles.com: www.goarticles.com

Buzzle.com: www.buzzle.com

ArticleCity.com: www.articlecity.com

SubmitYOURArticle.com: www.submityourarticle.com

Article Alley: www.articlealley.com.

ArticleGold: www.articlegold.com

Amazines: www.amazines.com

eBooks

eBooks are a good way to send your brand around the world with your visitors' distribution tools. If they like your eBook content and think friends or colleagues should get a copy, it is forwarded on without you even knowing. Viral marketing at its best. You can also use eBooks as an opportunity to convert visitors to leads with a form to capture their details. Offer them the chance to download the eBook, which has to be appealing enough to make them part with their email address, and then you have another string to your email marketing bow.

When we discuss email marketing in Day 13, you will see that this is a fine way to grow your mailing list. Create an eBook and sell it online using Smashwords (www.smashwords.com) or Scribd (www.scribd.com) or you can create one in Microsoft Word or Publisher and then use a PDF creator. iHubbub offers members the chance to upload their eBooks, check out www.iHubbub.com/eBooks.

 My Top Tip

While we are on the subject of eBooks, try using a Webinar to promote your eBook. Webinars are ideal for training, marketing a new product or service, promoting a new membership site, building a mailing list as well as many other uses. See my eBook for more webinar guidance at www.iHubbub.com/eBooks.

eMagCreator

eMagStudio is a really cool desktop application that allows users to convert PDFs into high quality, interactive page-flip publications that give your eBook the 'flipping' or 'page turning' effect. eMagStudio allows anyone with absolutely no technical skills to create impressive interactive publications. It can be used to create magazines, micro sites, newsletters, reports, campaigns or any other corporate communication that you wish to publish online. Take a look at www. emagcreator.com.

PagePlus

PagePlus has 1000s of professional templates, full import, editing and publishing with shape drawing, 3D graphics tools and effects as well as photo editing with over 70 fixes, enhancements, corrections and filters. You can also create your own high impact and elegant graphics and logos with drag and drop simplicity. Try it at www. serif.com/pageplus.

Text Aloud

I often read my written work out loud to myself because it helps to spot typos and grammatical errors. When I Googled to see if there was software that could do this for me, I found TextAloud. This dapper download reads text from email, web pages, marketing materials and any written work aloud from your PC. It is ideally suited for people with limited eyesight, but is a huge help to give your marketing materials, and in particular your eBooks, a prime polishing. I now use it for press releases too.

TextAloud offers a free trial with voices that don't sound too robotic. You can also purchase premium voices with English or American accents if you wish. Web owners and digital marketers will receive great value from this smart little tool. See how you can avoid publishing your eBook and other articles with typos and errors by giving it a go at www.nextup.com/TextAloud.

Summary

We've already discovered that there are a number of marketing tools available to increase traffic to your site. Today we met share buttons and other bookmarking options.

We also learnt the value of blogging as a key marketing tool. While blogs allow you to engage in a conversation with your customers, it also improves your website's search engine rank because of all the fresh new content going up onto your site. Get blogging as soon as you can, it is great fodder for those Google spiders and you may just enjoy adding content to your site this way. Try and make it a fun way to engage with your audience rather than a tedious task. We also realised that Article Marketing is a slow burn. I am sure you can see the benefits of a constant 'leak' to get your keyword-rich content onto other sites and benefit from links back to your site. While eBooks are similar to Article Marketing, they have the added benefit of helping you build a marketing database of fans who are keen to read more of your interesting content.

Both as a blogger and an article marketer, you can effectively build links, increase search engine ranking, drive traffic to your website, and establish yourself as an expert in your niche.

Today we also discovered that eBooks are a good way to send your brand around the world with your visitors' distribution tools. You can also use eBooks as an opportunity to convert visitors to leads with a form to capture their details and build a mailing list by offering them the chance to download the eBook.

Day 7
Video Marketing

Today you will learn:

■ Why you have to get onto YouTube

■ How to use video marketing to drive traffic

■ How to set up a video channel

Video now has a vital role so that web owners can be seen on every screen at home, at work and on-the-go. Techcrunch recently reported that 'video' is driving online growth and that in a few years' time, mobile video viewing is expected to be triple what it is now.

Platforms such as YouTube have given browsers greater access to the use of web video as well as increased marketing penetration for web owners. Video marketing is another essential avenue to increase 'direct traffic' to your company's website. You can do this by having highly desirable videos that help grow your video channel's subscribers and build inbound links into your website. Having fun and light-hearted viewing will develop your businesses personality and brand and increase awareness for your product or service.

YouTube

There are numerous video channels out there, but YouTube is the second biggest search engine in the world. Twenty-four hours of video are uploaded to YouTube every 60 seconds! Note that I previously said 'search engine' because it is not just a video site; people do normal searches on YouTube as they would in Google.

YouTube is owned by Google and is being classed as the 'new encyclopaedia'. This is because video isn't just for our 'entertainment', it's also changing the way we learn with users being able to create and distribute video content to inform and teach. The original founders, Chad Hurley, Steve Chen and Jawed Karim, knew that their peers were making and sharing social video and their core value was to allow users 'open uploading'.

Creating a YouTube account and uploading a video is simple. If you have a Google Account, you can link it to your YouTube account for easy access. YouTube will then automatically create a channel which presents all the videos you've uploaded.

Pros
- ✓ Video market leader
- ✓ Lots of third party add-on tools
- ✓ Good videos have potential to go viral

✓ Drives traffic to your site
✓ Gets your message across in a fun, friendly way
✓ Recruits new employees or builds company culture

Cons

✗ Fight it out with the many millions of competitor videos
✗ Expensive to ensure your brand displays well within a dedicated channel
✗ Not using YouTube will leave you at risk of being less shareable (on sites like Facebook) and less viewable (even iPads can watch YouTube videos)

"

HubSpot's Top Video Tips

1. Decide what type of video you want to create. The type of video that is right for your project depends on how you want to film your video and what the purpose of your video will be.
2. Decide on the format for your video. The format will determine the video's style. Will you film in HD for broadcast quality in case you get it onto TV? Do you want to record using a 16:9 (or wide screen) aspect ratio? Perhaps you will create a mini set, and use a tripod to film your video. Maybe you will hold the camera while recording. To help you decide, watch other videos to see what you like.
3. Set your video goals. Creating video is a lot of fun but, as with any marketing project, it's important to set goals for the video you produce. What do you want to achieve from your video?
4. Storyboard your video. Storyboarding is a technique to map out a video sequence prior to filming. In true form, a video producer would draw the scenes on paper as they would appear on camera. For marketing purposes, create a storyboard in written form to plan for your video's content.
5. Pick your topic. What video content should you feature? This could be a simple interview subject or a complex plot and storyline. Brainstorm the topic of your video.

6. Write the script. Once you've picked your topic, you need to write your script. If your video requires multiple shots, characters and scenes, script out your video in detail. Be sure to include the sets, stage actions and dialogue. If your video will be mostly conversational, create a list of bulleted notes. It will keep you organised during filming and save you time later.

7. Decide on your video's call-to-action. Too often, marketers leave this to the very last minute. Decide what your call-to-action will be while writing your script. What do you want people to do after they watch your video, for example, visit your site, subscribe to you on YouTube, watch the next video, subscribe to your blog and tweet your video? Be sure to connect your call-to-action with the goal you set for your video. It's also important to remove as much 'corporate friction' from your video calls-to-action as possible. If your call-to-action (or the video itself) is too corporate in nature, people will be discouraged from sharing it with their network, thus decreasing its reach. You don't want people to think your video is a commercial if that's not its purpose.

Top YouTube Tips

- Keep videos short – two minutes maximum – with a catchy first 10 seconds
- Avoid pre-roll credits, go straight to the content
- Use audio hooks, like 'Did you know ...?'
- Try a visual appeal where viewers wait to see what happens
- Create videos with a simple single message or punch line
- Make bold and challenging statements
- Get the titles and keywords right to ensure your content is found when viewers search
- Keep production quality as high as you possibly can

Toby Beresford's Top Tip

- A YouTube thumbnail is taken from the image at the middle point of your video.
- For a two-minute video make sure something interesting is happening at one minute.

YouTube Networking

Toby tells us that finding other publishers in the same category can be a good source of networking leads. There is a value for YouTube publishers to follow each other's channels as YouTube's suggestion engine factors this in to ensure their suggested videos are relevant. For example, if you publish videos on classical music, other classical music publishers may follow you and you should return the favour. Engaging with top YouTube stars can also help your cause. Asking them to comment on your video will also increase traffic.

"The key to success with any YouTube campaign is to keep content short."

Toby Beresford, Pailz

My Top Tips

How to get viewers:

- Use good headlines
- Tag your video with keywords
- Piggyback popular events – for example, there would be plenty of 'Christmas' searches in December

YouTube Optimisation

The screenshot below shows you how to optimise your YouTube videos. It is best to do this when you upload the video, but it can be done afterwards by editing your settings in 'my videos'.

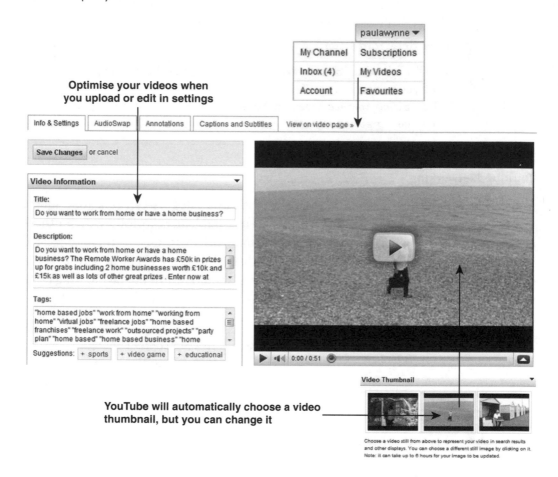

As you would optimise a page with metadata, do the same for your videos:

1. Click on my account > My Videos > Info & Settings.

2. Choose a keyword-rich title.

3. Ensure your description has keywords relevant and specific to your video. Remember to use primary tags or keywords.

4. YouTube will automatically choose a thumbnail for your video, but you can change it in your settings. Why not try out all three thumbnails for a few days or a week at a time, monitor viewings and see which creates the most viral views?

Promoting Your Video

Feature the video link on primary website pages, tweet and blog about your vids and even embed them into your site. Add a YouTube button or icon to your home page with links to your YouTube account or video. You can find a range of buttons and icons available by Googling 'YouTube icon' or YouTube button'. See the cool icon I found in the following screenshot.

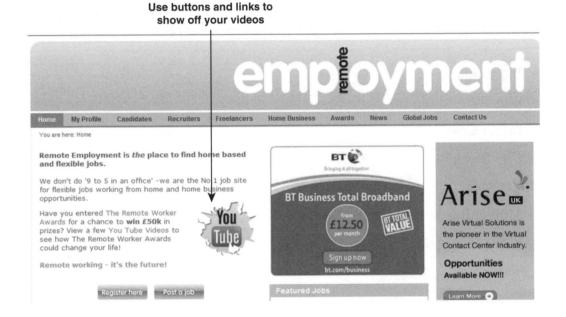

Use buttons and links to show off your videos

YouTube Resources

There are YouTube tools for:

- Saving and downloading videos
- Splicing videos and creating new content
- Keeping track of what's hot on YouTube
- Linking YouTube videos to accounts such as Facebook

A list of YouTube tools can be found at: www.quickonlinetips.com/archives/2006/10/the-amazing-youtube-tools-collection.

Check out YouTube Insights on your account. This gives you valuable information about who is watching your videos: www.youtube.com/my_videos_insight.

Other Tubes to Try

There are a number of other broadcast areas you may want to research as an alternative or addition to YouTube as well as other video resources:

Big Contact

Blip TV

Bright Cove

Clip Shack

Crackle

Motion Box

Podcast

Screencast

Spike

Twitvid

Viddler

Wild Voice

Yahoo!

Video Daily

Motion Vimeo

Camtasia

Thousands of people around the world use Camtasia Studio to create videos that train, teach, sell, and more. It's the easiest way to demonstrate a process, product or idea.

Camtasia's Studio is designed to be as intuitive as possible, so users with limited technical knowledge can easily create highly professional videos. You can record exactly what they see on your computer screen, including all visual elements, from mouse movements to data entry, with the option to add audio, such as a music track or a voice over, as well as web cam video. This 'screencast' can then be shared across all video tubes including iPhone.

Recording: The flexible recording options give you the choice to capture full screen, window or region. You can also add in music tracks, microphone, your computer's audio plus picture-in-picture with your video camera.

PowerPoint Plug-in: The toolbar inside PowerPoint makes it easy to record your presentations, either live or from your desk with one click. This intelligent technology also keeps track of where the action happens during your recording and zooms in on areas you need to highlight.

Editing: Once you have your content recorded, polish it up and turn it into a professional screencast with features such as call outs to focus the viewer's attention, cursor effects to help them follow the action, transitions to walk your audience through your content easily with title clips that introduce or divide your video, and captions that display text. The demo library is stocked with professionally-designed assets you can drag-and-drop into your video. You can then upload various video formats to YouTube. Take a look at www.techsmith.com/camtasia.asp.

Flip Video

Flip Ultra is an exciting and extremely handy little pocket camcorder, which makes shooting and sharing video simple and so much fun! The day I got mine, I had been in the garden and was constructing a hedgehog home – after finding one of these solitary creatures foraging through my flower beds for slugs and bugs. It was really cool to whip out the Flip and capture Hedgy scurrying around the undergrowth. I'm not suggesting that this is everyone's idea of good television, but it was fun and it was really quick to do with Flip. Imagine what it could do for your marketing campaigns. It now goes everywhere with me (the Flip, not the hedgehog!).

Flip Benefits

- Internal memory capacity 8GB, allowing you to capture up to two hours of footage
- Flip Ultra recharges via the flip-out USB arm, which connects directly to any computer
- Simple, one-touch recording and instant playback
- Upload videos directly to YouTube
- Capture still photos from your videos

My Top Tip

Take a look at the various ways I have used Flip in my YouTube videos (www.youtube.com/user/paulawynne) where you will see Flip's credits. Then sit straight down and get one from www.flipvideo.co.uk!

Windows Movie Maker

There are various ways to import video footage onto your computer. Once your footage is on your computer, a video editing tool, such as Window 7's Movie Maker, allows you to edit and upload your new video to YouTube. With a few clicks in Movie Maker, you can make movies from your videos and photos. You can also trim your video clips, add music and drag the soundtrack to the clip where you want the music to play. And then publish your movie on YouTube right from Movie Maker. You can automatically turn a bland video into a stylish movie with 'AutoMovie'. It adds themes, transitions, effects and titles in one click, turning an ordinary video into a movie. Movie Maker is only available on Windows 7: http://explore.live.com/windows-live-movie-maker.

Summary

With all the great and easy-to-use software now available along with handy cameras like the Flip you can't go wrong with video marketing. We have come a long way with digital cameras and camcorders so there is no excuse to avoid getting a video marketing channel. Even the simplest camera or camcorder will get you started quickly and easily. Brainstorm some ideas about what your video content can be or bounce ideas off students – they normally have some brilliant suggestions for this medium as it is fun and so on-trend for the younger generation.

In saying that, even old fogies aren't hard pushed to come up with some interesting ways to shoot a quickie video. Upload a variety of interesting videos and see how viral they can become. It's such a buzz to see your 'views' rising all the time. Even if you haven't actively marketed the video and just have a YouTube link on your website, the view count rises. Don't forget to optimise your videos as this can help your views and thus build traffic. My best advice: Play as much as you can with video, it's the easiest way to learn!

Summary

Day 8
Social Networking

Today you will learn:

- The difference between social media and social networking
- A brief history behind all the social media fuss
- Online versus offline networking
- How to use social media for business
- How to engage and build a network

When people start talking online, building relationships and meeting new people through people they know, the simplest form of online networking begins. Just like the old 'word of mouth', inviting your friends who then invite their friends' leads to an extensive networking circle. And with this came the social media explosion.

First, let's get the difference between social networking and social media clear.

Social networking is creating a web of connections between you and friends on sites such as Facebook, My Space, LinkedIn, Ning and iHubbub.

Social media is the content that you distribute. So it's about your content on blogs, Twitter, Digg and all social sites.

Think of it as a coffee break: The coffee cup or mug is the network. What you put in it (the liquid content) is social media. Online, you would do this by choosing your cup or 'network', which could be Facebook, LinkedIn or any others. Then you decide what social media content (text, podcasts, videos, etc) you will pop inside when you tweet, micro blog or post.

Brief History of Social Networking

Although social networking seems to be fresh and new, it has been around for decades and actually goes back to the early days of computers and the internet. It may have been outdated and almost 'ark-like' before the World Wide Web (www) really took off with mass appeal, but it was still a method for online communication.

Not so long ago, SixDegrees, Tribe, Friendster, Bebo, My Space were classed as the innovative 'new medium' sites until the 'F' word came along quite by accident. Mark Zuckerberg started a social network as a communication tool within his college campus to help students manage their social lives online. Blink . . . and suddenly Facebook has emerged as the world's largest social network. Watch the film 'The Social Network'.

> *"It must be real and engaging. All communication should encourage others to follow you."*
>
> Judith Lewis, Beyond

Most social sites started with different types of user-generated content, blogs, photo sharing and poking friends. But when Facebook introduced the 'Newsfeed', which allows people to find out what is happening in their friends' or business colleagues' lives, it resulted in the biggest complaint and criticism they had had up until that point.

However, although Facebook's newsfeeds started an outcry about privacy while sharing information, it soon caught fire and everyone realised its power and suddenly loved the idea. New sites were soon following suit, such as Twitter, which allows its members to spread mass messages with social sharing.

USER GENERATED CONTENT: If you offer your users the chance to add content to your site it is called 'user-generated content'. This can be blogs, comments, bookmarks, events, news, videos, podcasts, profiles and articles. It's a great way to increase traffic and visitor engagement while at the same time filling your site with valuable content.

With new sites springing up all the time, millions of people are now able to turn to social networking sites every day to tell the groups of people around them – in a sense their community – about anything from a family announcement to important business news.

To Be or Not To Be Social?

So what's all the fuss about social media? Social media is a new modern media stream, aimed at social interaction with a selected target audience. Fantastic publishing tools give you the ability to reach your friends and acquaintances through monologue-type conversations which turn into dialogues amongst your 'fans and followers'.

"More people are using social media to communicate."

Andrew Seel, Qube Media

Different people use social media networks for different things. Some use it for PR, marketing, and broadcasting their business message to achieve a viral effect for a concept. Others use it for socialising and interaction within a community. Even actors, authors and celebrities use social media networks to socialise with their fans. Okay, maybe that's not *really* socialising in the true sense, but it just goes to show the wide scope social media has to offer.

My Top Tip

If you want your website to be more social consider Open Source platforms such as Drupal Gardens or Drupal Commons. Acquia's social collaboration tools offer you the ability to increase social engagement on your site with community capabilities such as friends, streams, groups and calendars. Look at their product list on www. acquia.com or Google for other 'Open Source' social solutions.

So Why Network for Your Business?

Traditionally, networking is about offering advice, doing favours and generally building business relationships, which can be done online or offline. It can be a great way to promote your business and brand, and it offers a way to reach decision-makers who might otherwise be very difficult to engage by using conventional sales methods. It starts with referrals and introductions, either face-to-face at meetings and gatherings, or by other contact methods such as social- or business-networking websites. This progresses to personal relationships with potential clients to share best practice experiences with peers and competitors. Most networking, whether online or offline, is quick, easy and costs nothing but your time. No wonder networking is one of the most cost-effective marketing methods for developing sales opportunities and contacts.

Networking is often mistaken for hard selling and let me tell you, I hated offline networking until I realised that it *isn't* about selling. It is about people and building relations with them over a period of time.

> *"Social Media is, first and foremost, human to human interaction . . . You are the personality of your business."*
>
> Ian Dodson, Digital Marketing Institute

Whopper deals can be made at networking events, but it's important to attend a networking event without 'selling' as your only goal. The same applies to online networking. Until you understand this, you won't be comfortable in a networking environment. I wasn't, until it dawned on me that I was there to meet and get to know other like-minded individuals. With that weight off my shoulders, I relaxed and enjoyed myself and since then I have met some fantastic and fascinating people at networking events. Some of them are now involved in my business, advising me on my business journey, a few are expert contributors to my books and others have become really good friends and colleagues.

Remember the old saying 'Give and you shall receive' that our mothers used to drum into us? Well, my mum did anyway. Same thing here. Start networking with a 'giving' attitude and more than likely you'll walk away with some kind of reward. 'Givers get' is an oft-used expression to describe successful networking.

Online vs Offline Networking

To get started with networking, you need to consider what sort of networking you want – online or offline. Either way, you've got to be in it whether you like this sort of thing or not. The more exposure you can give your business and website the better, especially if your site relies on local or regional business. Before you embark on a social networking frenzy, think about your purpose in connecting with others online and offline. What are you hoping to achieve? How much time can you spend on this? It's easy to get carried away because the power to connect is at your fingertips. It is also important to remember that all your new online connections can be developed offline, and vice versa.

Online Networking

Online networking is now so common that it crosses over easily between social and business with professionals adapting to a specialised and social conversation without even thinking.

It can be highly irritating chatting to someone either in a meeting or socially, and then they start tapping away on their smart phone or laptop. Not so long ago that may have been due to an urgent email popping in, but more so nowadays it could be the result of a social networking ping from a friend or network connection. Texting, instant message chats, tweeting and even blogging by phone and laptop is so much part of life that it's firmly integrated into varying generations and across diverse cultures.

Online networks can be broken down into different categories. Some sites enable you to set up an online profile where you post activities, details of your business in directories (such as iHubbub's home working directory) or adding articles so they are purely profile building.

Other sites are support orientated where they offer help, knowledge, collaboration and skills exchanges for ideas and deciphering challenges. The most well-known sites are for communities to exchange conversations with other members and thus engage in networking, recommendations, referrals and online marketing.

LinkedIn is an excellent business networking site and has improved the way you can make industry contacts. Facebook is very popular because it's easy to use, but be careful not to mix business and pleasure. You can start a business group on Facebook which will help you to keep your personal life personal. Twitter has grown for both consumers and businesses and is even used for cultural and global events. Although iHubbub is essentially a community for home-based workers and businesses, it is also there to connect authors, freelancers and members to share advice and expertise. It has been developed out of necessity to help, support and encourage people with an affinity for this way of working. At the same time, it allows members to access thousands of contacts with whom they can network within the home working and home business world. There is an untold number of niche sites such as this. Stick around . . . we are going to discuss the most important networks and platforms to join in Day 9 with social media tools.

As the social networking revolution drives 'doing business' to new interactive heights, it's becoming more crucial for small businesses to join some of these social media sites.

The direct, instant accessibility of the web has opened the world up as marketing and publicity channels. Although Facebook started as 'a social scene', it is now a cost-effective way to engage a target audience and attract attention to your brand or online presence.

It's pretty obvious that the web is one big social place, where people have conversations, and connect and follow others. The old-fashioned 'word of mouth' has become 'word of mouse'. Joining conversations and setting up your own network with links to people and companies will form a vital part of your online marketing strategy. And you can monitor and track all exchanges with your network, whether it is personal or business.

Andrew Seel's Top Tips

- Be transparent
- Write what you know
- Have a conversation
- Add value
- Create excitement
- Be a leader

However easy and quick online networking may be, it should NOT be seen as a replacement for good old-fashioned offline face-to-face networking. Trust and credibility often comes when online networking is taken offline when people can get to know each other and build a valuable business relationship. People buy from people they like, so think of networking as building business friendships. Experts advise that an intricate blend of online and offline forms the most substantial networking connections.

Offline Networking

Offline networking is based on introductions, either face-to-face at meetings and gatherings, or by referrals.

Most small businesses start with no budget at all, so rather than be coerced into investing in printing hundreds of business cards for networking meetings, consider exactly what you need and what is relevant to your business. Getting your name out there and meeting people is invaluable and essential.

As with online networking, offline networking falls into different categories, from breakfast networking or lunches and dinners to speed networking. Let's face it, you can even network in a pub or school playground.

Some of the most popular offline networks are BNI, BOB Clubs, Chamber of Commerce, IOD, CBI, which all provide many different events and platforms throughout the year for their members. Remember to check out costs before you take the plunge. Also suss out the 'commitment', as some networking events can be pretty intense in that you must attend on certain days and times of the week to keep your place, while others only allow a certain number of attendees from each sector.

Most groups will allow you to join as a guest or non member, either for a limited period or at an extra cost while others are free at all times. It is worth investing your time by visiting to see which one suits you. Also, be aware of referrals you may have to make for other people. This is great when it works, but be careful you are not spending valuable time finding work for others and lose sight of your own goal.

A few networks might insist that you bring a friend, while others ask you to 'intro' the person beside you. All this may be too daunting for a first timer, so find this out before turning up, paying a fee and then escaping to the loo in order to avoid something that makes you uncomfortable.

Talking of the loo, don't miss a good opportunity to make contacts. This is somewhat embarrassing, but for some strange reason I feel the need to share it with you. I was at a recent seminar and quickly realised that so many of the people there were ideal for iHubbub as they were experts in their field and could provide training webinars for our members. I waited eagerly for the speaker to give the audience some kind of opportunity to intro themselves.

None came. By the first coffee break, I darted into the loo along with a multitude of ladies. As I was drying my hands I suddenly had this crazy thought and didn't wait for it to manifest itself and cause trepidation in what I was about to do. Instead, I spun around and fired off a quick 'Hello Ladies'. Before I knew it I was asking this long line of ladies waiting to 'powder their noses' that if they were experts, coaches, trainers or specialists in any field to please grab me and hand me a business card.

Well, let me tell you, I quickly became known as the 'Loo Networker' and it was only later that the reality of what I had done hit home. Needless to say, I left with stacks of business cards and have since made great connections with some brilliant people with a delightful assortment of expertise. So the moral of the story is to never let a great networking opportunity slip by! Both offline and online. Check out my eBook on offline networking for more juicy titbits of offline networking (ihubbub/eBooks).

My Top Tip

- Prepare what you are going to say about yourself and your business in a compelling way
- Practise the ease with which you connect with people
- For offline events find an easy ice-breaker, such as 'Have you been here before?' or 'Did you have to come far?'
- Take a look at the network lists at iHubbub.com/networks for some ideas of what networks to try

However you decide to network, you need to make sure that it is relevant to you and your business objectives, which could be business development, scouting for new clients or simply meeting new people in your sector. You should always match your objectives to the network you are thinking of joining and check what benefit it has to offer.

As well as being ideal for sales opportunities, offline networking with the right group of people allows you to form or forge personal relationships with potential clients, and tell others about your fabulous new site and all its benefits. It gives you the ability to give back to that particular community in some way.

Judith Lewis' Top Tip

Linking everything together where relevant will significantly help your social media profile.

Summary

We have certainly covered some social ground today. Just a quick reminder that social networking is the platform where you meet up and network (aka the coffee mug) and social media is the content you put out onto various sites (aka tea for you and hot choccie for me).

Although social networking seems to be new, it has been around for decades and now may be the right time for you to climb on board. We discussed how to get started and what sort of networking – online or offline – is best for you, but try and get an even balance of the two. You need to be connected to what you are most passionate about so find a community that matches your zeal. And of course, you do this by connecting to what is 'possible' inside yourself and then finding the place or network that makes things 'possible'. With this attitude, the more exposure you can give your business and website the better.

Once you have been through the next section on social media tools you will be prepared to start building relationships via conversations and thus creating a following on your chosen networks. Always remember: networking across all social network platforms is a combination of good content and frequent interaction with others.

Day 9
Social Media Tools

Today you will learn:

- [ ] Why you should be 'linked in'
- [ ] The difference between Facebook and fan pages
- [ ] How to use Twitter and the jargon that goes with it
- [ ] Ways to manage and monitor your social media
- [ ] What apps will keep you on track
- [ ] How to build a following
- [ ] Why you need a social media strategy

Now that you're up to speed on the importance of networking we can start playing with the various social media tools. You will soon realise that social media (SM) forms a sizeable chunk of your online marketing, therefore it's important to spend today thinking which social sites you will use. Social media tools and techniques are spreading fast and furious so today we'll uncover the secrets of how to use the key tools. We'll also explore the various SM apps and aggregators to spread your messages and conversations across multiple social platforms, and to monitor and track your conversations along with your follower's discussions.

 An **aggregator** is a website's software technology that collects and organises (aggregates) previously defined information from the online world. This can be in the form of news, reviews, searches, jobs, videos and survey data.

Planning your social media strategy may at first seem like a maze. There are so many things to juggle when running your own small business and limited resources won't help the barrage of emails, blog posts, tweets, vlogs (video blogs), videos and bookmarking you need to keep up in the air. It can be too easy to just set yourself up on a load of networks, and then struggle to get the most from them, because you don't quite know what you should be doing. Our experts advise that the first steps for setting up a social media strategy is to decide which tools are most suitable to your site.

LinkedIn

LinkedIn is all about business networking as this is a B2B environment with conversations that tend to be focused around business topics and solutions. It's an invaluable business tool for connecting with new business professionals, finding new team members and joining groups. This means that it tends to be utilised by some as a 'rolodex' of contacts they have made over time. It is often used to find new employees, check on people pre-interview, find event speakers, source relevant conferences and more.

"Grow LinkedIn contacts organically through business transactions or after face-to-face meetings"

Toby Beresford, Pailz

You can integrate LinkedIn to your browser toolbar and even into your Outlook contacts. The Outlook plugin saves you time by notifying you when Outlook contacts update their Linkedin profiles. Judith maintains that you should first connect with people who you have met in person and remember to reference where you met them – and expect occasional rejection. Once you have begun to build connections, you may choose to ask or answer questions or participate in other ways to build connections. Also consider employers, employees, suppliers, and past work colleagues for connections.

Pros
✓ Protects you from unwanted business calls while still allowing meaningful business transactions to take place
✓ Good for checking out companies, their staff, etc
✓ Broadcasts your updates to your groups or connections
✓ Particularly useful for finding new business customers, investment or leads if you are targeting the business community

Cons
✗ Fight it out with many millions of competitors
✗ Could be a duplication of contacts in your database
✗ Be careful not to spam your network
✗ A slight barrier to linking social profiles

"LinkedIn is 'huge' for professional networks – the bigger future player in the professional world."

Anthony Quigley, WebKitchen

LinkedIn Groups

There are a number of groups you can join on LinkedIn. These groups can help you connect, give you relevant formation and offer opportunities to share news and notes or answer and pose questions. People set up groups for all sorts of reasons, but mostly because they want to share experiences, knowledge and discussions within a selective industry sector. Talking to other members within such groups can certainly help your cause or business and at the time cement connections that may become firm business relationships in future. Only start a group if you have an affinity, passion and energy for a given topic.

> **Toby Beresford on LinkedIn**
>
> After any business transaction send a request to add the person you met.

LinkedIn Dos

- ✓ Ensure you connect promptly
- ✓ Include where you met the person in the contact request
- ✓ Connect with current colleagues as well as past ones
- ✓ Contribute to a community
- ✓ Update your status to ensure a business focus

LinkedIn Don'ts

- ✗ Don't use it as a social tool
- ✗ Don't set up a group or community around an idea, blog or sport

Facebook

Although Facebook started out as a social site it has fast become the premier online marketing tool. A Fan Page allows you to keep your Facebook business activity separate from your social activity, but if you do set up a Fan Page be sure to update it regularly and consistently. It is important to keep your social messages in line with your brand so think before you post! The purpose of any post or message needs to be clear before engaging in any social media campaign or project. Put yourself into the mindset of the participant and ask yourself 'What's in it for me? Why would I "like" or join this community'?

Pros

    ✓ Use Facebook to track down old business acquaintances and reconnect with them

    ✓ Can be leveraged by B2C brands more easily than those who need to work within the B2B business space, or are developing business-targeted social media campaigns

    ✓ Ideal for targeting and reaching a broad consumer audience

Cons

    ✗ Can't necessarily see what people are saying about your company – most conversations are kept private between friends

    ✗ Tendency to be spammy, so don't accept 'friend' requests unless you know them

    ✗ Social media campaigns will fail if you target the wrong community.

Key Facebook Features

Let's go over some of the key features and terms that you will come across when you venture into Facebook.

Facebook Profile: A normal Facebook page is based on an individual and enables you to connect with your friends online.

Fan Page: Generally used for business goals, and often dedicated to a high-profile individual, celebrity or something that requires interaction to connect with millions of fans. For example, when creating a meeting space for people interested in chocolate, a Fan Page could be made for the blog, but a Facebook group would be made for the generic concept of chocolate lovers or a love of chocolate.

Groups: This is a tool to engage with other Facebookers with conceptual ideas not tied to a specific business. For example, there are lots of common interest groups such as writing groups, social groups in which people share common beliefs and goals and even extreme groups where members are passionate about topics like conservation, the environment and specific cultures.

My Top Tip

To give your brand an identity on Facebook, create a 'group' or 'fan page'. Click on the Advertising link at the bottom of your Facebook home page or go to either: www.facebook.com/pages/create.php or www.facebook.com/pages/learn.php.

Wall: If you have used Facebook before then you'll already know that you can send messages to your friends, connections, colleagues and fans by publishing a 'wall post'. This wall post will then be distributed to all your fans who see the post on their Facebook home page and they can comment on it or 'like' it.

'Like' Button: When you click on the 'like' button on a webpage it automatically goes into your stream and alerts your Facebook friends that you liked a page, business, person, idea or interest group. 'Like' buttons are automatically and easily set up by Facebook. All you need to do is copy and paste the code into your web page after you add a few details to this link: http://developers.facebook.com/docs/reference/plugins/like/.

Andrew Seel on Fan Pages

Andrew suggests you should analyse why you want to set up a Fan Page before going ahead.

1. Think through the reasons and why people would want to join your Fan Page. What's the point of it? Is it to build strong relationships with customers? Or promote a product or service?
2. Think of a real-life situation as if you were hosting a party, to help you decide what content and images to include. You should have an active community manager to get it moving, based on what you are trying to achieve.

> **3.** Build in the time and resources to reach out to tell people about your Fan Page and why other people are enjoying it. This gives you the opportunity to talk with your community, and gives fans reasons why they join.
>
> **4.** Don't set up a Fan Page just because it is freely available. Think of it this way: if you had to pay a huge fee for a Fan Page, would you still do it?

Facebook Dos

✓ Automate a few micro posts or news feeds each week in a SM aggregator
✓ Feature products and events and share them with followers
✓ Engage in a group conversation by asking and answering questions

Facebook Don'ts

✗ Don't create a purely broadcast account as these quickly lose followers; instead, get into conversation with your fans
✗ Don't rush in and create a Fan Page unless you have the bandwidth to keep it constant, fresh and alive with info
✗ Don't automatically connect with every friend request as you may be be spammed, which becomes a real pain!

My Top Tip

For more information on how to use Facebook Pages, see HubSpot: www.slideshare.net/HubSpot/a-visual-guide-to-b2b-facebook-pages-4277600.

Toby Beresford's Top Tips

- Have different lists with different interest groups in your Facebook account.
- You need to see these as actual groups of interconnected people rather than as one too many mailing lists.
- Ask group members to check the group wall and communicate with each other.
- To avoid your mail outs appearing spammy, ensure they are about the shared issues of the group.

Last Word on Facebook

Using Facebook for marketing can be tricky for many businesses as so much activity is invisible, so it's best kept as private conversations between friends. However, by building a fan base around your brand, you can feed your site's content into those conversations. It is always good to keep your digital plans at the top of your mind when using Facebook. Although it is the third most-used website globally (after Google and YouTube), it may not be the ideal network for your site. Use it to publish regular, mainstream, Facebook wall posts and offer incentives for people to connect with your site or business. And use your groups to email others with similar mindsets.

Most consumers, 'pro-sumers' and businesses gain advantage over their competitors by using this phenomenal growth 'machine' so determine what you need from a network and then use it to your benefit.

Twitter

As well as a real-time network to spread and share information to keep on top of what's happening in your social networks, Twitter is a powerful marketing tool, with 'follow us on Twitter' buttons fluttering across most websites.

So what is all the fuss about? It is often described as a 'real-time' information network that connects you with friends, colleagues and unknown followers. It allows you to keep up-to-date with subjects of interest and groups of people that you want instant access to on a daily basis. Why would you want to be connected to unknown followers? Simple, they may find what you do and what you tweet about interesting and thus want to keep up-to-date with what you have to say. Tweeting is all done by short, snappy 'micro-blogs' or snippets of a conversation. Think of it as a tiny synopsis of a bigger story.

Pros
- ✓ Good for breaking news and following trends as they happen
- ✓ Adds value to followers
- ✓ Retweeting good content spreads your site fast
- ✓ Celebrity twitterers are helping Twitter go mainstream

Cons
- ✗ Reach is one tenth of Facebook
- ✗ Easy to lose followers
- ✗ Restriction to 140 characters – not every business can achieve this concise messaging
- ✗ Lacks story-filtering ability of Facebook so can result in information overload

Twitter Jargon

This list of terms used in the Twitter world will help you to become a real 'twit'.

Tweet: A message posted in a box on a user's profile, which is limited to 140 characters.

Follow: Hitting the 'Follow' button allows you to see all of a user's posts and shared information in your stream. Twitter offers suggestions of people to follow and you can search for anyone who may be on Twitter.

Stream: Microposts from people you are following will show up in your timeline or stream.

@ Replies: A tweet that contains someone's user name, preceded with the '@' sign. These are used to attract the attention of an individual and are only visible to people who are following both you and the person you're addressing.

Judith Lewis' Top Tip

The best way to involve others is to be a part of the conversation; only use @ replies when you have something personal to contribute.

Direct Message (DM): DM is used when you want to have a private conversation with another Twitter user.

Hashtags: A tweet that includes the hashtag (#) before a particular word or phrase allows anyone to participate in a discussion around a particular topic and is commonly used for conferences, hot news topics and recurring Twitter trends. They help twitterers to find information about events, topics, groups or 'tribes', and any other interests. Every tweet that includes the hashtag just before a chosen topical word can be found simply by searching on a hashtag phrase. To use a hashtag, first check that it is unique and noone is using it. Do this by searching Twitter and then tweet your chosen hashtag among all the people you want to participate in that particular conversation.

My Top Tip

Be careful not to muddle DM direct messages with @ replies or hashtags, as you could end up sending a private message out publicly by mistake!

Andrew Seel's Top Tips

- Choose buttons depending on your audience
- If they are active in Facebook, use a 'Like' button
- If your audience is using Twitter, use a retweet button

Retweet (RT): This is when you repeat a 'tweet' from someone you follow to your own followers. Although mostly used for business, Twitterers tend to RT people who mention them in a positive light. You can simply click on the 'retweet' link next to each post, or implement retweet buttons on your web page with a 'Tweet Me' widget.

My Top Tips

- Make sure links are valid
- Use bit.ly to shorten links
- Ensure your tweet is less than 120 characters to allow space for others to retweet it
- Try different retweet buttons, as some may make your page load slower

Twitter Dos

✓ Use good copy to introduce the link to encourage other users to retweet your message
✓ Provide value – be it *your* thoughts or someone else's
✓ Automate a few tweets at the beginning of the day, which allows you to have an ongoing presence whilst you work
✓ Engage with followers by responding to any replies, checking your stats and participating in conversation at any time

Twitter Don'ts
- ✗ Don't just tweet about yourself or mundane things
- ✗ Don't spend every waking moment on Twitter
- ✗ Don't go over the 140 character limit – it will cut off the end of your message and make it look unprofessional and tacky

Once you have established yourself on Twitter, it's important to maintain your presence if you are going to make an impact. All our social media experts agree that you should tweet regularly and often if your followers expect it. The great advantage of micro-blogging is that you can produce lots of mini stories fairly easily.

Your Social Media Strategy

Now that you are familiar with the key social media tools, you can start thinking more clearly about your strategy. Firstly, you need to establish where your target audience hangs out by thinking about your website goals and objectives. Decide if you will use consumer or business language in your content and then select your social media platforms. This needs to be planned in advance before setting up your profiles.

Now you can start building relationships via conversations. This said, always try to be natural, honest and show your personality. You have to be prepared to be in this for the long haul, as creating a network of people to follow takes time. If you struggle with being social, why not brainstorm conversation ideas?

Engaging Others

Toby states that being part of the conversation is crucial to engaging others. To engage others you need to follow and contribute to the conversation which tends to be around what is new. If you offer a new perspective then others may 'retweet' or 'like' your post and share it with friends. In this way your content can cascade across the social networking world.

"Use free tools such as 'social mention' for monitoring Social Media and a RSS Reader like Google Reader or Net Vibes."

Andrew Seel, Qube Media

The people you follow will show up in your SM streams, so it will be much easier for you to interact and 'talk' to them in real time. Once you are following each other, it's just like a real-life conversation, except that the world can hear so be careful what you say.

 SOCIAL STREAM: As a stream of water is a current that rushes down a river bank, so a social stream is a wave of content that populates your various social sites.

Andrew Seel on Joining a Conversation

1. Comment on a blog
2. Engage on social networks
3. Respond to posts, tweets or blogs
4. Ask and answer questions on forums
5. Review and recommend products (not yours!)
6. Rate videos and images
7. Contribute to a wiki
8. Reuse and link to content

Building a Following

The more your posts are retweeted or liked, the more people will follow you. People want to get as close to the source of the news they are interested in as they possibly can. By being the authority in a niche area, the first to break news on the topic or the first to create the best conversation around breaking news, you will gain a following as people 'tune in' to you on their own social networking feeds.

"Publish personal, interesting information, add thoughtful content to conversations and retweet other people's tweets."

Judith Lewis, Beyond

For maximum success, follow the journalists' mantra 'Always Be Breaking' – breaking news is what spreads fastest, so be the one to break it. Whether it be about a new dot.com start-up in your area, the latest celebrity gossip, or what's happening in your village, people may want to follow you because they hear it first on your SM channel.

My Top Tip

Most social networks allow you to send a personal message to add or connect to friends. Always personalise this request and give them something that they may remember you by, such as: 'you may remember me by xyz'. For example, someone may send me a message reminding me about networking with them in the 'loo'.

Creating a Large Network

Networking across all social network platforms is a combination of good content and frequent interaction with others. When networking, it's worth doing your homework to identify the people who matter most in your area of importance and then cultivate a relationship with them. A mention or post from a top blogger can quickly result in several new fans or followers. Toby believes that in order to grow your network, it is key to offer your fans exclusive content – games, news, discount vouchers and downloads that are not available elsewhere. Ideally, the content should be related to the network you are using. His ideas include creating branded games that fans can play with their friends.

Quick Social Media Tactics

Here are seven hot tips to get the most out of Social Media Marketing:

1. Set up social media platforms that match your audience. For example, if your visitors are 'mature mind sets', don't start with MySpace. Try Twitter, Facebook and LinkedIn.

2. Promote and market your website through thought-provoking and valued conversations.

3. Don't use blatant selling messages. We all hate spam.

4. Title your social media platforms with primary keywords.

5. Make conversations captivating so followers want more. SM is about *talking* to your audience, not stuffy sales pitches.

6. Find your voice by being yourself; add humour, personality and interest.

7. To ensure best results, make sure your social media pages mirror your brand and personality.

Be aware that social marketing can completely consume your life. There are so many social media platforms to choose from, it's important to work out which one is best for you and why. So before you rush out and set up too many networks that you can't maintain, you should consider all the options before deciding on your strategy.

Managing Your Social Media

Some of our experts advise that twice-a-day (or daily) tweets or posts to your network is about the minimum to be seen as active. However, this can be exceptionally difficult to achieve if you are juggling many digital marketing balls – especially if you are a start-up or one-person business or web owner. It's no use hearing experts tell you that you have to tweet every day or so many times a day and you stress about how you will fit that into your extremely busy digital marketing life.

Find your own way to engage with others within your own comfortable level. You can always increase it as time permits. I find daily posts 'OTT' when there are other important tasks to juggle. I also believe it's about what you have to say. I prefer not to say, tweet or post anything that is just chatter or not of value. Personally, I don't want to know about people having a morning jog or how their dog 'pooped' when out on a walk. Thus I wouldn't dare do the same.

The essence is to decide for yourself and judge what you feel is important enough to tweet about. If you wouldn't want to read that kind of information in anyone else's profile, don't do it in your own. Don't use social media platforms just because it is the 'done thing' or think you have to tweet or post to keep a following. Tweeting, blogging and posting can be a huge time hoover and, rightly or wrongly, I prefer to post 'value' rather than constant 'chat'.

Apps to Keep You on Track

At the time when Twitter was really taking off, I remember thinking that it would be helpful to have an application to automate tweets, blogs, posts and social conversations across various networks. And, hey presto, soon some techie gurus were launching apps left, right and centre.

Social Media Apps are designed to automate blogs, posts and tweets, organise your lists into categories, set up groups and track how many people have clicked on your social network links.

HootSuite

HootSuite allows you to post to Twitter, Facebook, LinkedIn and WordPress in one go. HootSuite gives you the option of choosing a design theme and you can feature different social streams with a variety of tabs and columns . . . just fly over to HootSuite and see for yourself at www.hootsuite.com.

HootSuite allows you to schedule messages

Automatically shorten or
shrink URLs

paulawynne Please share these videos on how to win fab prizes in
our awards: http://ow.ly/22FPO.
2:52 PM Jun 24th via HootSuite
Retweeted by 1 person

Sent to Twitter

Tweetdeck
Tweetdeck is a tool that enables ease of view of multiple accounts including search results, direct messages and hashtags. It's useful for aggregating your information because it syncs with Twitter, Facebook, My Space, LinkedIn, Google Buzz, Foursquare and with an iPhone app. Find them at www.tweetdeck.com – Tweetdeck is now owned by Twitter.

Tweet Adder
Tweet Adder automatically builds targeted Twitter searches, auto follow, auto unfollow, auto tweet, auto message and Twitter trends. They're at www.tweetadder.com.

Su.Pr

Syndicate your content to StumbleUpon (a discovery engine or search engine that finds and recommends web content to its users), Facebook, and Twitter with one click with Su.Pr. It also allows you to identify the optimal times to post and schedule as many posts as you like to Twitter and Facebook.

Twitalyzer

As Google Analytics will track and record all your web hits, Twitalyzer will do the same for your tweets – completely FREE for all users. All you have to do is sign in with Twitter: www.twitalyzer.com

Monitoring Social Media

There are a number of companies that offer SM monitoring services, some are chargeable and others are free. Their software crawls over the web to monitor and track your social status.

Google Alerts

You can keep an eye on your online presence with Google Alerts by simply logging into your account and adding keywords to 'Google Alerts' to monitor all mentions on the web about you and your site.

My Top Tip

Use HubSpot's tool to track, analyse and filter your emails from Google Alerts and Twitter: http://alerts.grader.com.

Sprout Social

I have only just discovered this site and have already fallen in 'geeky' love. With only a few weeks under my belt, I haven't stopped playing with this fantastic online tool because it features so many ways to manage your social media. Let's take a look at the features:

1. *Organise your social networks*: One handy place to store all your information and data to make meaningful connections, measure success and know exactly where to spend your time. There are conversations taking place that may be relevant to your business across the web and so here's the chance to bring it all into one place, allowing you to listen, engage and build loyalty to grow your network. You can manage your Twitter, Facebook and LinkedIn profiles for multiple identities (you and your business profiles) in one great-looking dashboard. Here you get to track conversations, engage followers and stay up-to-date. Of course you can retweet, DM and reply to any message in any of your social network streams. It even gives you a breakdown demographics of male and female followers as well as their age groups. And it shows you an engagement and influence and score. Even though it could be a tad worrying at first if your scores are low, use this feature proactively to build your social media presence.

2. *Find and make new connections*: The advanced technology allows you to search for highly-targeted prospective customers and influencers based on criteria you define. Using location, interests and profile information, you can find these highly-targeted contacts. Search by keywords and location to find people who are likely to follow you back. You can suss them out quickly with a snapshot of their profiles and then add them to your list. For example, if you have a sushi bar in London, you can search 'sushi lover' located in this area and get in touch with them with information or special offers.

3. *Manage social contacts*: This CRM (Customer Relationship Management) keeps track of all of your communication history, user profile information, notes and reminders. In Sprout Social you get to create an entire profile on followers, including their company, position, email address and phone number. Each profile will also include links to their social media profiles and the ability to send them a message. This interesting software takes SM CRM to the summit.

4. *Monitor your brand*: Tweets, reviews, blog posts and news are all tracked. Your Sprout Social inbox hunts down all conversations, incoming messages and alerts

about the profiles you set up, be they business or personal, in an interactive stream. Your inbox allows you to filter contacts to easily find the information you are looking for – all in a chronological timeline. And, listen to this, it allows you to spy on your competitors to compare their social influence and engagement. A startling discovery if yours is low and theirs is high, but use this clever stuff to learn and improve your own social media content across many different networks.

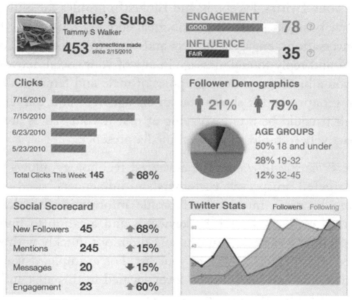

This image shows the wide range of management tools available in a Sprout Social dashboard.

5. *Measure success*: You can capture and measure data right in your browser or export to PDF format for sharing with business partners or colleagues – in intuitive, colourful charts and graphs. This is handy to track the impact of your social media marketing campaigns for feedback on your social media strategy in a variety of preset or custom date ranges.

6. *Track locations*: Track Foursquare and Gowalla locations to see analytics of customers or clients checking in to your business. It shows your most loyal customers, your high-traffic days and first-time visitors. When visitors are checking in to your business, you can easily connect with them to get their valuable feedback. You can also see what people are saying about your location and use the settings to receive email or SMS alerts every time a user checks in to a location. Like Remington bought the company when he loves the shaving blades, I'm using this dynamic software at www.ihubbub.com/ihubbub-social.

Free Monitoring

Take a look at the following free tools that help to monitor your SM (find the URLs at the back of the book):

Addict-O-matic

Board Tracker

How Sociable

Same Point

Friendfeed

UberVU

Social Mention

Surchur

Icerocket

Summary

Social media tools range from taking out a Facebook Fan Page or simply registering with Facebook, and tweeting your fluffed-out feathers on Twitter. You cannot and should not dive into every social media platform just because it is freely available.

Instead, go back to your strategy and consider each platform for its merits before setting up a trial run. Although we chatted today about the main networks such as Facebook, Twitter and LinkedIn, there are loads of other great networks to investigate to find out which is best suited to you and your site. If you're a new start-up, remote worker or home business, give iHubbub a go or pop over to Ning and see what's happening there.

Start to track and monitor your SM campaigns and use the variety of apps to start conversations. Some of the tools discussed today combine tracking and monitoring as well as giving you the ability to send out posts, tweets and blogs. Trial them all to see which you fancy the most.

Social networking, and social media with all its trendy tools, can be intertwined simply and easily within your overall marketing mix as well as your email marketing messages and reputation management. Talking of which . . . let's get stuck into that next.

Day 10
PR

Today you will learn:

- ■ The best way to manage your online reputation
- ■ Why you should plan and create a PR strategy
- ■ The best ways to gain media attention with free exposure
- ■ How to create a proactive PR campaign
- ■ What is newsworthy and how to unearth great story angles

I love sharing and swapping ideas to publicise a website. My background lies in PR and Marketing and like thousands, if not millions, of small businesses, Remote Employment and iHubbub had no advertising budget. Instead of sitting back and waiting for the media (and visitors) to just happen upon our site, we reached out to them.

Today, we will go through various aspects of PR, promoting your website and exploring inventive ways to increase your traffic through publicity. You will learn how to find a story in your daily business life – human interest stories that attract the media – and how to optimise that story and get it out there. More important is to have fun flaunting your knowledge and expertise by showing your passion and energy for your sector, product or service.

Public Relations

PR is all about creating goodwill for a person or business and maintaining that public image. Essentially, a PR Officer manages business and website communications. Online PR examines social media and all other internet channels to build a rapport with mainly the public at large, but also customers, employees, management teams and even investors or non-executive directors. There are many other aspects to Public Relations, but we are going to concentrate on reputation management, media relations and how publicity can drive traffic to your site.

Online Reputation Management

Reputation Management (RM) is the tracking and managing of your reputation on the web so you are prepared for good and bad conversations. The internet is all about 'free speech'. It's easy for people to be a reporter, critic and advocate, yet there is no control of these 'citizen journalists'.

We all know that bad news travels fast, but it travels even faster via the net because it doesn't go through an editor or publication's controls; therefore, it is harder to fix if things go wrong. Search marketing, social media and offline media all influence your online reputation. Andrew tells us that, traditionally, Reputation Management was reactive, hierarchical and defensive with a media-driven agenda to react to a crisis. However, he believes the rules have changed and it is now positive and proactive to build up goodwill. The most important aspect is to build a great reputation and optimise it for search.

"Reputation management is about building a good reputation rather than defending a bad one."

Andrew Seel, Qube Media

Andrew Seel on Reputation Management

By listening to online conversations about you and your brand, you can 'map your audience' to maintain control. Follow this guideline to create a Reputation Management Strategy.

Monitor:

- Unhappy customers
- Brand champions and influencers

Create and optimise all content:

- How does Google see and represent you?
- Google success is more than just your name
- Optimise all your content for search

Engage:

- Be transparent

Defend:

- Are you prepared for a crisis?

The most common problems for a negative online reputation occurs from outdated information, customer complaints, false accusations, haters or trolls, scandals and acts of God. Andrew believes you must be ready, with a trained team and an escalation plan, in case of a crisis.

> **Judith Lewis on Reputation Management**
>
> Those drunken tweets, pictures of the office Christmas party, video of a faulty product or blog about how someone hates your company will damage your reputation. Unlike in times gone by when today's news was tomorrow's kitty litter liner, today's blog posts are tomorrow's damaged reputation, possibly lasting for years.

Creating Your Escalation Plan

The most important aspect of an escalation plan is to respond quickly. Research the situation and check the facts, for example, is there merit in the comments? You need to provide the facts and ask for corrections as well as offer to discuss the issues. You can respond on your blog or within your social media channels. It is vitally important to work closely with all parties, keeping everyone informed and do remember to be honest, transparent and to listen at all times.

How to Respond

- *Where?* This is ideally done wherever the comment was posted. If it was on a blog and they refuse your answer, note this, and post it on your blog instead.
- *When?* In as timely a manner as possible. Most often this will be when it has been investigated, but do keep in mind that 24 hours is a long time on the web!

PR Strategy

Before we delve into the ins and outs of publicising your business, it is time for you to decide on your PR strategy. Focus on your business objectives and you WILL see traffic results. And you may even become an industry expert in the eyes of the media. You can create a constant flow of publicity into your business with a focused plan. Although the first and most basic steps are outlined below, your loaded plan, brimming with all the essential PR tools, will be evident after the next few chapters.

Step 1: Boiler Plate

No, you haven't fallen into another book about engineering. You have landed on the Editor's Notes or Notes to the Editor, also known as the 'Boiler Plate'. This is a summary at the bottom of your press release about you and your business in one or two brief paragraphs, showing why you are the right person to be talking to the media on that particular subject. The reason I start with this first is that being able to summarise yourself or your business gives you the chance to think about the key reasons why your message is important to this particular journalist or editor. It highlights your credibility, gives short sharp bursts about you and is, in a sense, a snapshot of your business.

Editor's notes are intended to be brief, but you also include relevant facts and other information that may not be contained in the release so do be careful to not bang on and on with too much detail. Give your media centre URL (for example: www.ihubbub.com/Press-Office) and let them browse in there instead. The editor's notes should also give details of how to contact you. I always include a landline, mobile and email address as well as website URL.

Step 2: Key Message

Plan your key message(s) and make notes about what your PR objectives will be. When we launched the Remote Worker Awards our main point was to draw attention to the awards for both employers and individuals.

This changed as the awards campaign moved towards deadline and with it our key message became to highlight the different award categories and then show off the finalists and winners.

Make your meaning memorable with your tagline and don't be afraid to show how you want to be known. I would go so far as to state what you are 'famous' for. With iHubbub we show how the site was developed specifically to help SMEs as we are in the same shoes. We highlight the importance of this community. Firstly, because it is the first social network for home-based workers and secondly, because of the huge growth in alternative working lifestyles.

Ensure clarity in your PR so that people get it in an instant. When we tell people we founded iHubbub to champion remote and home working, they get it straight away. There is no head scratching, frowning or eyes wandering as the brain tries to make the connection.

> *"Be creative, but truthful."*
> Alex Johnson, Journalist

The media aren't there to promote you, they want value and good content for their readers – so to get noticed you should highlight what extras you can give them. If you are launching a new product or planning an event, your key point will be the launch: why, how, when, where and what. After that it will focus on the success of the launch and the subsequent impact on your audience and market.

For example, after The Remote Worker Awards Ceremony there was an official release from BT as the sponsor as well as individual winner's releases to local and regional media, which detailed how their win would impact on their business. In the case of the people who won a franchise or website, we spoke about how their life would change as a result of winning this award.

So, your key message can change through your PR cycle, and by defining this from the beginning it helps to target the right media to ensure publication.

Step 3: Target Your Media

Look through your local papers or specific publications and magazines. Set aside some time each week or month to do a bit of research into the type of articles that appear in the media, who is writing about what, what's hot and what's not, look at the various topics affecting your industry and then decide if you can add value to these publications. Prepare a pitch or press release that may only need slight tweaking and can be used in a flash.

Whenever I set up a new campaign for a client, one of the first steps is to research journalists to prepare a list of publications to target. This could be anything from technical journals to business blogs or chatty consumer magazines. Go back to Day 1, 2 and 5 where you stepped into your visitors' shoes; think about who they are and what they read, then make notes on what kind of publications you need to reach in order to find those visitors. It may be only local and regional, but if your product or service is available to the world, why not go global? Yeah, this could be scary at first, but don't let the big wide world hold you back. If that is what your product needs, write it into your strategy.

You would, of course, start with the immediate media and then slowly spread wider and wider until you have time and resources to cover a global media audience. For example, iHubbub may be international, but we'll focus on UK media first, before spreading the news across the globe.

"I just want to know what the story is. The human touch is always the best."
Alex Johnson, Journalist

Timings and Deadlines
Publications have different deadlines so remember to check this out when planning your campaigns. Here's a guideline on submission deadlines.

- *Magazines*
  Generally, magazines work months in advance – in the middle of the year or just after, an editor will be hunting for Christmas stories and features. They are planned far in advance, researched and written up, ready to go to press at least

a couple of months before publication. For example, aim to send out Valentine releases between October and early December. A general rule of thumb – the thicker and glossier the magazine, the longer the lead time.

- *Newspapers*

   (a) Locals, Regionals and Weekly

   Depending on the frequency of the publication, deadlines may vary. For instance, a local weekly newspaper's deadline may be at the beginning of the week for a Thursday or Friday publication day, but they may also have inserts which require an earlier deadline.

   (b) Nationals

   Most national newspapers are daily and therefore news is far more instant. They also work with various inserts and as a result they will be working to several deadlines each week and even each day. A quick call will sort out the exact deadline for the publication you are targeting.

- *Broadcast*

   TV and radio move extremely quickly when receiving a press release of interest, so you may be invited in for a guest spot at the drop of a hat. Be ready!

My Top Tip

Sign up for media alerts so that the media comes to you for specific requests. Check www.ihubbub.com/publicity-club.

Step 4: Create Angles

Thought leadership and good quality content are buzz words so try and include valuable advice in your releases or pitches. This will help prove your expertise and the journalist will come back for more. It's fun to brainstorm a variety of different angles. If your product is seasonal you could choose different times of the year to promote different aspects of your business. Get your year planner into action and write down all the possible events and then diarise to get the release into the media in advance.

For example, have events on your year planner that are specific to your site. This can include seasonal events, such as Valentine's Day. For promoting my books, I have a variety of events from book festivals to start-up expos.

Also, find angles that you can use creatively to attract the media. For the second year's Remote Worker Awards, my goal was to get TV exposure. So I set about looking for the most unusual home business in our entries to make sure I would get the media's attention. Finding two unusual cases – one worked remotely from a beach hut, another worked from a World War II bunker – we arranged a video shoot and uploaded it to YouTube. After sending a press release to regional TV media, ITV Meridian picked up the story and gave us a fabulous piece over a period of two weeks right across South East England! View the videos on my YouTube Channel: www.youtube.com/user/paulawynne

Step 5: Media Relations

After deciding which publications or individual journalists are most relevant for your industry expertise, consider how you can build a relationship with them. They may not bother at first, but don't give up. Keep building these media relations and they will call you when a need arises.

Before I became an author, I had a very good relationship with my local media as I was constantly showing my determination to get my books published and my films produced. I found all sorts of different angles. Then a client, who couldn't crack this particular publication (despite it being their local newspaper), asked me to help, I was able to get loads of coverage on the strength of my past relations with their editorial team.

Do be careful, though, don't annoy them to the point that they tell you to go away. That is not part of your strategy, so give it time and, as the saying goes – good will come to those who wait.

> **Fiona Wright on Media Relations**
>
> - Don't just let them know about your fantastic spa, resort, vineyard or restaurant – invite them for a press trip experience.
> - Send them samples, make them feel good. They won't say something is good if it's not, but they will, at least, write about it.
> - Make sure the story you give is exclusive to that particular publication. You can pitch the same thing with different angles to different magazines, but journalists get annoyed if a rival magazine or paper has the same story.
> - Journalists are human beings. Their job is often stressful and dull. Cheer them up, make them laugh or give them something interesting and they are yours for life!

Step 6: Q&A

Prepare a draft Q&A by thinking about the answers before writing out the questions. In a sense it is working back to front. It also gets you into gear for future media requests that may come your way. If you are actively pumping the PR machine it will keep you in good stead to stay focused.

When writing a Q&A, start with your bio, it gets you in the groove and thinking about the focus. For example, when I started working on this book, I considered what questions would be asked and what answers I would provide. The most obvious seemed to be 'What's the book about?' So I wrote my answer. Next up comes 'Why did you decide to write the book?' Then 'Who is the book for?'

I could even have questions like 'What principles did this book reinforce for you?' and 'What information did this book reveal that you believe the book's readers will not already know?'

Do something similar with your Q&A. You know the answers based on the features and benefits of your site, so come up with thought-provoking questions, such as this one at the end of my Q&A: 'How do you envisage people applying this book's information in their everyday business?' See an example of this in my online 'Media Centre'.

> **Fiona Wright on Gaining Media Attention**
> - Be your brand
> - Be available
> - Be honest

Publicity Matters

As a publicist for your site, your key responsibility is to construct publicity campaigns for your product or service. So, what is publicity? It's a planned and calculated promotion to create news. This could be to drive traffic to your site, product or service, increase brand awareness or generate sales leads. Go back and check your goals and objectives so you can decide what you want to achieve.

Free publicity, either at a local or national level, is the perfect way to kick-start your business. The media look for news stories, not marketing messages, from a company, so you need to create a news story and make sure it is newsworthy. For example, you could support a local charity event and tell the media about your fundraising.

Case studies can also be effective. Find someone who uses your services with a good story to tell. For example, Babyworld found a mum whose husband was serving in Afghanistan and so they created a story about how their online community of mums provided her with a willing and friendly support network while her husband was away.

Finding PR Angles

There are tons of positive angles just lying about waiting to be found, and in a sense, you'll become a PR hound. There is no doubt that PR can be a cost effective way to bump up a staid and traditional marketing strategy. Best of all, you can do it yourself.

Start by organising your facts and find answers to 'The Five W's': Who, What, When, Where, Why and make sure you add in How, too.

- Your story should be unique and newsworthy
- The event must be current – old news doesn't tick boxes
- Try to identify what the editor is looking for, they are constantly swamped with press releases so your good story must jump out at them
- Run a poll or survey to gain feedback from real people – this makes a meatier story
- Keep in your industry's loop with newspaper and magazines stories

 My Top Tip

Try setting up a poll or survey, which is easily done through online polls and surveys. Find some that offer a free trial to see how it works. Don't try and stuff in too many questions, just the important ones.

So, in a nutshell, decide on your PR angles and then tailor your story with your human story, which of course can be sent to different publications depending on the outlet's target audience.

Use this list to find a direction for obtaining low cost or free publicity for your site:

- *Anniversary*: Be proud of your established business, but don't go down the boring lane of age-old anniversary announcements. Find ways to tell the media that you are so good in what you do and thus show your established time in business. Also learn other inventive ways to use anniversaries.

- *Commend* someone for a good deed and show your human spirit.
- *Charity:* Commonly used, but it can be effective with an innovative approach. Rather than giving money, which is boring and may not be newsworthy, why not support a charity with a startling device or human interest idea?
- *Column*: Approach the media to write a regular column of advice on your chosen topic. Make sure your passion and energy shine through rather than any commercial 'selling' messages.
- *Competitions*: An old classic, but still extremely effective if you discover novel routes to market a competition.
- *Current News*: Keep a watch on the news to source stories you can piggyback.
- *Mistakes*: We're all human, so use mistakes to benefit your site. You can't hide away from them, instead be open and honest.
- *Price War*: Tread carefully here, price wars can be damaging and only use this if you know it will be to your advantage.
- *Problem Solving*: Can your product or service solve a specific problem for someone that will be newsworthy? If so, give it a go.
- *Tour*: Conduct show-rounds of your warehouse or product house, especially if you have some interesting characteristic to show off.

My Top Tip

You can see more publicity ideas in my eBook on Free Publicity on iHubbub: www.ihubbub/eBooks.

Don't just listen to my publicity ideas, here are some from the horse's mouth . . . er, journalists' mouths.

Fiona's Free Publicity Tips

1. Do a poll with stats to create a buzz around your business, for example if you're selling a lip salve – '7 out of 10 women hate the way their men kiss them'.
2. Piggyback a popular story in the press.
3. Do 'a guide to' or put up 'experts' to produce press stories.

Alex's Free Publicity Tips

1. Set up your own micro site on the internet, such as a blogging site.
2. Ask everybody you know who blogs if you could do a guest blog for them.
3. Find websites that cover the same subjects as your specialism and make interesting comments on their posts.

MICROSITE: This term refers to either a single web page or a few pages meant to be an 'accessory' to a website. They can be used to add special information on a given topic or for promotional purposes such as extended details on events or editorial articles.

My Top Tip

Daryl Wilcox publishes white papers that I recommend reading. Download these great guides at www.dwpub.com/whitepapers

What is Newsworthy?

Let's face it, not all news stories are worthy of being read. To ensure your press release is not just dumped in the bin before being fully read and understood, learn how to tick all the editor's boxes. They want valuable, indepth content that makes a good story. Imagine you're a journalist writing a story for your local paper. Read 'your' release through their eyes and ask yourself – will it hook you (the editor) and make you (the editor) care? Will it be compelling and interesting enough to readers?

"Send in your release, but make it worth our while or it will be binned immediately."

Fiona Wright, Journalist

The Human Touch

Bloggers, journalists and editors will always want to find out more about YOU or your site's PEOPLE if you feed them titbits of information that spark their interest. Think about how you came up with the product in the first place or why you are offering that particular service. If you are stuck for ideas, mull it over and dig down to help an inspirational story rise to the surface. Remember, even a product launch or random business service has a human behind it.

My human interest behind setting up Remote Employment is twofold. Firstly, as a mum I always wanted to work around my son's school run and after-school activities and couldn't find a site that offered home working options, so I freelanced for a long time to fit in a lifestyle of choice.

Secondly, my partner, Ken Sheridan's human angle is as a 'corporate Dad'. He has a long history in marketing fast-moving consumer goods such as the Tetley round teabag, as well as being one of the inventors of a space age water cooler. He also worked on brands such as Pepsi and Monster Munch and spent a lot of time travelling, yet he wanted more time with his sons. So a home-based business was ideal. Like Ken, if you have fascinating stories on the products you've worked with, find a way to weave that into your PR, even if it is only a one-liner or a reference to what you did previously.

For example, I often refer to Ken as the man who helped launch Tetley's round teabag. If I introduced him as just a man who has a business that is doing such and such . . . how flat does that sound? Whereas the notion of a round teabag launch conjures up all sorts of images for any tea drinking nation.

So what? Who cares? The caring comes when you dig deeper and reveal the person behind your site. Always remember the human interest. Keep telling yourself – there is a human behind every story. I am not suggesting you 'wash your linen' in public or do anything that goes against the grain or even reveal secrets you shouldn't. Not at all! Believe me, I am an extremely private person even though I advocate PR. All I am saying is, look behind your 'business story' to get the human angle. If it is interesting and warrants a good read that could inspire others, the media will want to know about it.

Summary

PR is an innovative way to promote your business. Now that you know that PR is essentially all about creating goodwill for a person or business and maintaining that public image, you need to keep the lid on your reputation by tracking and monitoring what people are saying about you online.

By setting up a PR strategy from the outset, your PR campaigns should complement all the other digital marketing initiatives we have learnt so far and help you gain free publicity for your product offering. Your job as publicist for your site is to keep coming up with new and innovative publicity campaigns for your product or service.

Today we also discovered that there are so many ways to gain valuable free publicity. Following the horde of PR tips above is bound to get you noticed in your local and regional media. Spend some time going over the different story angles suggested today as this will encourage a journalist to get in touch with you. Remember to include the human story and be sure that it is newsworthy or run the gauntlet of being tossed onto the editor's pyre!

Besides, it's fun to brainstorm a variety of different angles and add them to your year planner. It's even better to be asked by a journalist to contribute to their article so check out media alerts and iHubbub's media calendar. Let's get cracking and reveal the host of PR tools in Day 11 to leverage your PR strategy.

Day 11
PR Tools

Today you will learn:

- How to write and optimise a press release
- Why you need an online newsroom
- How to distribute your news and pitch to the media
- The best ways to find and build media contacts
- What to do when you have the media's attention

As I mentioned yesterday, today we'll be taking your new-found PR knowledge and combining it with the latest PR tools, goodies and gadgets. Your PR toolkit consists of distribution techniques for ensuring your release lands under the right editor's nose. We'll also go over pitches, photo calls, media interviews, press kits and which media databases to use. But let's start with the first PR tool – a press release. This is a key tool in getting your story, PR angle or publicity event in front of a journalist or editor.

Press Release

A press release is a notice or story sent to the media with the aim of attracting their interest and gaining valuable editorial space in their publication. A press release can be sent directly to your chosen media contact or through a newswire or PR planning service. Your press release should be well-written before you submit it to the media.

> **Fiona Wright on Press Releases**
>
> Journalists hate lists and hard work! Use your imagination – the more work you do, the more attractive it is to me. Grab my attention, but don't send me puffed-up stories or stupid gimmicks.

Preparing a Press Release

Before we get started on writing your press release, take a few minutes or more to think about what you want to achieve:

1. *Goals:* Why are you trying to get news coverage? What do you hope to achieve? Do you want to increase traffic to your site at the same time as getting media attention? Do you want to sell products or your services? Do you have a big event, conference or product launch?

2. *Media:* Which media will you use? Choose from local, regional, national, specialist or global media.

3. *Audience:* Who is your ideal target? Are there several different target audiences? Know your visitors, what they read and where they hang out, so you can find them through the media they read and visit.

4. *Language:* A B2B or B2C audience? This will determine if the language should be business and corporate or chatty for consumers.

5. *Timings:* Is this for an event or product launch? What are the timings? How will they affect your release and news coverage? Confirm the publication's lead times to check you don't miss any deadlines. Go back to your PR strategy to remind yourself of media deadlines.

> **Alex Johnson on Press Releases**
>
> - Always have an angle.
> - Journalists want stories, ideally exclusive ones, which sound good or look great in pictures.
> - They don't want dull press releases which simply say how fantastic you are.
> - Get to the point quickly and leave email and phone details.
> - And they don't want to be bombarded. If they don't run with your story this week, they won't next week, and if you badger them then you'll go on their blacklist.
> - Ensure that the journalist you contact actually writes about your area too.

6. *Research:* Do you need any research or stats? Have you got all the correct facts to hand? Is there anything else that would or could add value to your release?

7. *Images:* Are there any stunning shots you can include with the release? Include a human angle in your releases and add a head and shoulder photograph.

8. *Press Kit:* Is your press kit ready? Prepare your press kit before your release so you can get the feel for how to approach your media needs. It will also help you to focus on your message and goals.

9. *Social Media:* Don't forget to add your social media links to all your press releases and in your online press room.

10. *Clients and Visitors:* Include your clients, customers and visitors when you send out releases. Send them all your news and you may be pleasantly surprised that some may lead to enquiries or even sales.

How to Write a Successful News Release

With over 10 years of experience in the online news and press release distribution industry, PRWeb believe they have a unique understanding of how to write a news or press release so it achieves success online. Their downloadable tips to help you write a professional, concise and powerful news release include proofreading, and writing professionally with concise words and a strong active voice. They also advise starting strong with a first paragraph that clarifies your news, to stick to the facts without using industry jargon and to not be afraid to toot your own horn.

 My Top Tip

Have a look at this link which gives clear details about how a press release should be laid out: www.prweb.com/pr/press-release-tip/ anatomy-of-a-pressrelease.html

Your Press Release Template

Use the following tips to grab attention.

1. The Headline or Title

This is probably the most important part of your release as it is the first thing the readers will see and thus it will determine whether or not they continue reading:

- Hook the reader and capture their imagination with catchy, short, snappy headlines
- Use positive headings which will stand out
- Don't use spammy words such as 'free' in the title, find alternative creative words

2. Opening Paragraph
Another vital aspect to your release is to outline the story angle and summarise the whole story in order to highlight the key points:

- Use the five Ws: Who, What, When, Where, Why and don't forget the How
- Don't give a sales pitch!

3. The Layout
- Quote the person in the story
- Quotes from experts will add authority and impact
- Tweak for different media
- Keep to one page if possible
- Always include contact details

4. The Writing
Write in the third person, so no 'I' or 'we', instead 'they' and 'she':

- Avoid jargon, techy terms, corporate language and abbreviations
- Back up your claims with stats
- Show references to facts or figures

5. The End
- Make it clear where the release ends with a bold 'Ends'
- Add your 'Editor's Notes' and contact details

Alex Johnson on Press Release

Editor's notes should have contact details and a brief rundown of genuinely useful information. Don't send pages and pages of background history and information. A journalist can find that or simply ask for it.

How to Optimise Your Release

Optimising your press release is the same as On Page optimisation, except on a slightly different scale. So, when we chatted in Day 2 about focusing on your primary keywords in the first few paragraphs on your page, you should do the same for your press release.

Through this, Remote Employment managed to get loads of back links to our site and build both traffic and awareness through our PR campaigns. The awareness came from the media attention we were grabbing and lots of different publications up and down the country covering our stories. By optimising our releases, this doubled the impact of the publicity by driving traffic back to our site.

Key Point 1

Use your best keywords in the first paragraph and hyperlink each keyword with the most relevant page on your site. Remember 'relevant' and 'specific' as the optimal focus. The landing page link must be related to the keyword you are using as well as the context of the paragraph in the release.

Key Point 2

Don't overdo the links and get 'link happy'. If you send it out through a newswire service it may not be picked up if it has too many keywords links as Google will think you are spamming.

Key Point 3

Over the course of this book, we have explored several ways to get into your visitors' shoes. Once again, we hop into their boots to find out what they want from you and discover what their problems could be, so you can tailor your press release to deliver the solution. Include the terminology that they would use. Think, speak and write like your visitors. All too often, PR people get fancy and show off their industry knowledge only to find out that their audience has no idea what they are talking about.

Online Newsroom

Your online newsroom will send a clear message to the media; they will know you are serious about your PR, your press coverage and your media contacts. Some websites might also call this news, press room or media centre.

By adding all the information the media need, you are showing how important and valuable they are to your site. In a nutshell, this will include your bio, high-resolution photos and photos of your products or event.

Creating an online newsroom is a great way of allowing journalists and editors to write about your business without an interview from you. It also gives them access to this information around the clock. Often journalists are given a story at the last minute and during their late night research they can hunt through your online newsroom to find what they need.

My Top Tip

Your media centre or press room is another great place for optimisation and for search engines to find you with all the rich keyword content that oozes out of this online room.

A newsroom is a good way to demonstrate professionalism to both the media and any visitors who want more info on you before buying from you. Seeing a list of press releases or news clippings establishes that you are trustworthy and will deliver your promise. Show off broadcasts, podcasts or videos and quotes. You can even suggest ideas for stories if you want to share them.

"I like to see samples, case studies, statistics in a press kit, and someone available on the end of a phone 24/7"

Fiona Wright, Journalist

What Your Media Room Should Contain

1. Bio
Give a brief bio similar to your article resource box and editor's notes.

2. History or Stats
Include the history of your website or a quick summary of the background to setting up the site along with any research or related stats.

3. Key People
Do remember to include all your key management or people involved with the site by adding a quick paragraph and image of them.

4. Image Gallery
Images of you or your product are essential so find a good photographer who will do some headshots of you and possibly a whole photo shoot of your products. When you do submit pictures, ensure you offer the best quality cropped images you have. If your budget is stretched, try using a student photographer or a freelancer.

My Image Top Tips

- Crop images up close and personal, preferably a head-and-shoulder shot cropped tight to remove unnecessary background. Blur it out if your camera has the ability to do this or zoom in on the people.
- Avoid busy backgrounds, mirrors, windows and glass which cause reflections.
- Hone in on the action in the image – remember 'humans' are the centre focus.
- With firewalls so tough on spam today, you have to find a way to allow these images to get to the right media. If you have stunning products or places to show off, don't scrimp on this area.

If you end up having lots of products or images that are necessary to show off to the media, consider adding an image gallery in your online media centre. I have done lots of work for hotels and restaurants, and if they don't have any good shots I always recommend a photo shoot and add the beautiful photography to the newsroom so journalists and editors can access them at their leisure.

> *"If I like the story and the human interest, I'll ask for anything I want afterwards. So get everything ready, but don't send it all to me at once."*
>
> Alex Johnson, Journalist

5. Releases
Show off your press releases in your newsroom. They more you have, the more there is for potential customers and journalists to read about how wonderful you are. A simple link will suffice.

6. Clippings
Don't forget your press clippings or online news coverage links. If you attract lots of media attention you should proudly show this off to everyone who comes along, but do be aware of the NLA [Newspaper Licensing Agency] regulations.

7. Events
If you have events, or if you exhibit at shows and run conferences, the media may be interested in attending.

8. Reviews
Journalists will be interested in what you have to offer your customers so why not create special demonstrations or trials for a journalist to test your products. You can even go one further and include a registration form for the media. Or add a button or link for them to receive a product in return for a review.

> *"Newsworthy items are essential for an online newsroom. Not old stories just there to fill in white space."*
>
> Alex Johnson, Journalist

9. News Coverage

It is important to show how newsworthy you are by including all your clips and media links. Create a separate page for this and include a link in your media room so journalists can see what other publications are saying about you.

10. Case Studies

Journalists love case studies. If you have any on your site, include links to them in your press room.

11. Contact

Lastly, but certainly not least, don't forget to add your contact details, including your mobile number. If you are determined to get into the media as an industry expert, you need to be at the media's beck and call. The media works all hours of the day and so should your press kit!

Online Press Kits

With the media working all hours, consider using a press kit tool such as PressKit 24/7, which keeps your information and press details organised by providing links that can be accessed all the time. InstantMediaKit is another service that doesn't take long at all to load your online media kit with all of the marketing materials you need to make a great impression. Have a look at www.presskit247.com, www. instantmediakit.com and www.mediaroom.com. They do charge, so decide either that you can do this yourself or use them if their service is superior.

News Wires

A news wire is an online service that sends your press release to newsrooms, websites, radio and TV stations and other media outlets in a chosen country or worldwide. It's the quickest way to get in front of a large media audience. By using a news wire or news distribution service, your story can get picked up in the national press as well as by local and regional papers and you may even get featured on talk shows.

News wires are extremely effective for global publicity as the internet has been active in helping news to quickly travel greater distances. Google 'news release distribution' or 'news wire' or 'press release wire' to find stacks of sites offering this service.

 My Top Tip

There is a multitude of online press release submission sites. It may be a tedious task, but multiple submissions will lead to lots of back links if your release is properly optimised. See my eBook for a long list of them (www.iHubbub/eBooks).

Google News

Another way to get your release noticed by the media is to set up a Google Sitemap. Check these techie notes about Google news submission: http://www.google.com/support/news_pub/bin/answer.py?answer=74288.

The aim here is to make sure that there is always lots of fresh news to get indexed on Google, the sitemap URLs and news must be only two days old. If this is a steep task to deal with, you can submit your news release to iHubbub. Our home business social network helps members to get their stories into the news through our Google Sitemap. Our Members News Page features the latest home working news and stories from home-based businesses so it is a portal for journalists to pick up on news from home businesses around the world. Add your news: www.iHubbub/members-news.

Media Contacts

Another ideal way to get wider coverage and easy distribution is to use a PR planning service, which gives you round-the-clock access to media databases and on-going distribution rather than a one-off.

"Build media relations gradually and sensibly. Make them relationships, not just contacts in your Blackberry."

Alex Johnson, Journalist

These software resources provide easy systems to get in touch with journalists. Apart from the news wires, you can also send press releases out through this type of service and access the provider's database of media contacts. They all offer different subscription packages with a variety of PR tools and is largely dependent on your needs and most of them offer a free trial.

FeaturesExec Media Database

FeaturesExec is an 'up-to-the-minute' online database of media in the UK and other major European markets. FeaturesExec helps PR professionals and small business owners to become media experts by providing constantly updated editorial contacts and 'forward features' information on thousands of media outlets. The main benefit is to search for media contacts in any sector and choose any media type, from blogs to specialist publications. You can use these contacts to target regional outlets for geographic PR campaigns and be one step ahead with forward feature opportunities.

Magatopia

Magatopia is a free online service featuring a wide range of magazines in the US. Browse at www.magatopia.com to find relevant magazines for your PR campaigns.

Media Finder

Media Finder seems to be the largest online database of US and Canadian magazines, catalogues, newspapers, newsletters and journals, and operates a subscription-based service or a digital download option.

Their comprehensive database gives two ways to find the right media for your campaign:

1. *Keyword Service:* Enter a keyword or select a category and hit submit. Double click on the first title on the results page to view the types of data returned, which shows more than 30 fields of data.

2. *Targeted Lists:* Select one or more items from each field you need to define your search. Be sure to check out the many tabs on offer such as staff, circulation and print spec. You will then get a count of the results to obtain the number of titles you desire. After submitting payment you can download the results in standard formats and open them in a spreadsheet. Fields include publication title, either in company name if you are looking for a specific publication or company type if you want a general overview of what is available.

Publication details feature category, frequency, publication type, target audience and media type. All these are extremely useful for a targeted campaign. The address search comes in a city or country drop down if you are aiming at a particular US or Canadian location. The last field you can use to search for media is called 'Must-have' and shows items such as email, phone or web link.

CisionPoint

CisionPoint PR software weaves together the essential PR tools in four easy steps. Firstly, you *plan* your campaign and create distribution lists by searching a huge media database finding thousands of outlets and contacts – including blogs and bloggers – around the world. Secondly, you *connect* to these journalists and editors by sending releases either through a personalised email within CisionPoint – you can also send a test to yourself for one final typo check – or you can use the inbuilt web and wire service. Thirdly, you *monitor* the press clippings and online coverage in order to finally *analyse* the results with tracking reports for multiple campaigns to see what's working and where. Check out this great PR tool at www.uk.cision.com

Photo Call

A photo call is generally only used if you have an event, a product launch (in my case, a book launch) or another major reason why journalists should show up to take photos of you. Nowadays, though, with digital photography so advanced, most publications will ask you to provide a good head and shoulders shot or a high resolution image of the event.

Interviews

If you get an interview, be ready with your pitch, but also prep yourself with suggested questions they can ask you during the interview. This is where your Q&A comes in handy (take a peek at my books' Q&As in my media centre), but be sure you can answer all of them with clarity and focus. No bumbling allowed! If you get an interview, practise sound bites or keywords – this can be in the mirror or on your own, but is best done in front of your partner or a family member who can give you good feedback.

If you are dead keen and can't wait for an interview to come along, go after them. Find the host or producer of a radio show or a journalist doing similar stories and get in touch with them. Firstly, acknowledge their work to show you have done your homework and give them your best pitch. Be skilful about working your name, website or business title into the interview conversation, without being obvious about it. Always refer to the name of your site or product instead of just saying (especially in a radio interview) 'my site' or 'my book', for example. This way you reinforce your hard-working brand.

Industry Expert

To get media coverage on your topic, you obviously have to know what you're talking about – but you don't have to be the world's foremost expert in your field. The other aspect to consider is that most people take what they know for granted and therefore don't consider themselves experts.

Almost everyone knows a lot about something and could be a very useful resource to a journalist doing a story on that subject. The media love experts who can talk about a wide variety of topics and therefore are more likely to get placements.

How Do You Know if You Are an Expert?

Follow your heart on this one. Only you know what your capabilities are and what expertise you have to offer. More than likely you have something good to offer others. You probably have lots of valuable information and knowledge between your ears that you may not consider as expertise. Many small businesses, web owners and home- based businesses don't realise the potential they hold as an expert to the media.

What Do Experts Do?

An expert provides information, comments, experience, expert skills, specialist knowledge and analysis on news subjects, current affairs and specialist products and services.

What Are the Benefits of Being a Media Expert?

You will have the opportunity to gain media coverage for you and your business – you may get national media exposure which will cost you nothing other than time. While building news stories for your business or website, you will increase credibility and boost your PR campaigns. Of course, it will also raise your profile's exposure and work to find new clients and cement relations with current clients.

Who's Searching for Experts?

The media are constantly on the hunt for anyone who can help, advise and supply expert knowledge on specialist subjects. TV and radio researchers often invite industry experts and opinion leaders into their studios for live broadcasts on a variety of subjects. National newspaper and magazine journalists who require information or comments on forward features and planned editorial calendar topics are always on the hunt to find expert knowledge and skills on topical issues or relevant subjects. In other words, the media could be looking for you!

The media are looking for:

Qualified Professionals: This includes lawyers, doctors, consultants, surgeons, accountants, financial advisors, architects and many other experts in the professional field

Academics: Professors, lecturers, senior researchers

Official Experts: Professional bodies, trade unions, industry, business, political parties

Spokespeople: From associations, institutes, guilds, societies, charities, campaign groups, religious organisations, research centres and sports authorities

Individuals: Including business entrepreneurs, consultants, musicians, entertainers, actors, performers, sportspeople, writers and authors

Could You Be an Expert?

As shown above, an expert is anyone with either the specialist knowledge or experience in any subject that might be of interest or value to a journalist, editor or anyone in the media and media-related industries. They often need information, comments or advice and may invite you for an interview for a news story or feature. Before you tell yourself you don't fall into this category as being an expert – stop! Fear of being rejected and lack of confidence will keep you in the doldrums. Everyone has more 'gold' inside than they realise – be brave and show off yours!

My Top Tip

iHubbub features a list of experts in a variety of industry sectors and we are always on the hunt for experts to give training webinars to our members.

"You'd be amazed how far offering to pay for lunch will get you."
Alex Johnson, Journalist

PR Pitch

Prepare a short, simple pitch that is to the point and is in with your keyworded message. It is a synopsis or snippet of your business, product or service. Use this pitch in any networking meetings you have, and keep it handy to fire off to any journalist who sends out a media alert. Or if you find a good article to which you'd like to contribute your thoughts and ideas, send your pitch to the journalist and acknowledge his or her 'fab' article. Only send the pitch by email with a link to your press kit or your press release; if the journalist wants more, he or she will contact you.

My Top Tips

Have short, sharp answers to these questions:

- Why me, why now?
- Why should they care?
- And why do they care now?
- What makes you so special?
- What is unique about you that will interest their audience?
- Remember all the W's.

PR Pitch Guide

Use this pitch to guide you before you make any calls:

1. *Who is the pitch about?* Human touch, story angles, what is unique or special about the pitch?

2. *What are you pitching?* Reasons for the pitch, what is the pitch about?

3. *Why are you pitching?* Unusual info, why should they care?

4. *Where?* Special event, odd story, locations.

5. *When?* Why now, timings, deadlines?

6. *Media to pitch to?* Which media, what target audience do you want to reach, specific media contacts, national, local or regional, specialist media?

Media Alerts Top Tips

Here are my top tips for pitching to editors and journalists through media requests:

1. Tailor each alert with relevance to what the information the journalist is requesting.
2. Build relations by asking if there is any other information you can give them.
3. Ensure you give value for money with good quality story ideas or content.
4. Show human interest behind your PR campaigns – journalists want the human angle!
5. Ensure your website press page and online profile is up to date and complete.
6. Provide a good case study as this could help their story.
7. In the first instance send a brief email in response to a request. If they ask you to ring, do that instead. If you don't hear anything in a week or so, follow up with a friendly reminder but don't nag. Journalists are generally working on several stories and articles at once.

Media Requests

Media requests from journalists and editors bring media pre-publication enquiries right to your door with requests from the media, journalists and editors who want to find specific information. It gives you the chance to provide material for their story. Each enquiry is a potential media coverage lead, so the service is a great way to generate publicity and raise the profile of your organisation.

Response Source

Response Source is a media service that delivers pre-publication enquiries from journalists who are researching features to PRs across all sectors. This gives you the chance to provide material for the story. Each enquiry is a potential media coverage lead, so the service is a great way to generate publicity and raise the profile of your organisation.

US Media Requests

If you are in the US or if you want to crack the American market, try using an alert system. The best ones I found that focus on US media are:

- Pitch Rate: www.pitchrate.com
- Reporter Connection: www.reporterconnection.com
- Haro: www.helpareporter.com
- Reporter's Source: www.reporterssource.com
- BloggerLinkUp: www.bloggerlinkup.com

Be Ready for the Media

When you are given a pop at being in the media, take it. Drop whatever you are doing to take up the opportunity they are presenting as it will pass far too quickly. I missed an opportunity to be on the LK Show. Lesson learnt: If they ask you to come in tomorrow and your diary is full, say 'Yes, of course' and then move the meetings. Don't say you can only do next week. Next week won't cut the media mustard.

When they get in touch, be responsive and get back to the journalist immediately. If he or she wants more info, do a call around if you have to find case studies, ideas, research or suggestions. Always make the journalist's job easier by giving them everything they need. It will only help you to get the story that you so desire.

> **Fiona Wright on Media Relations**
>
> - Be charming and patient!
> - Be available 24/7 – there's nothing worse than not being able to get hold of someone when you're on a deadline.
> - Offer help, even if it's not directly related to your business or product – journalists never forget a favour.
> - Don't nag or harass – journalists will avoid you and not take your calls
> - Don't get upset if your product or article doesn't appear – often it's beyond the control of the writer.

Awards as a PR Tool

Being a finalist or winning a business award is an excellent way of gaining PR as well as recognition and credibility for your business. This takes time to perfect and before you do anything you need to identify which awards are most likely to benefit your business. If you're good at copywriting and you take the advice in the next few pages, your award entry can stand out from the crowd.

Benefits of Entering Awards

As well as being a great way to gain PR for your business, there are other benefits to entering awards:

- Pride, immense satisfaction and motivation
- Boosts confidence and morale
- Helps to scrutinise and evaluate your business
- Impresses customers, clients and colleagues
- Gains recognition and credibility
- Demonstrates passion and belief
- Strengthens your market positioning

- Gains publicity and new marketing opportunities
- Endorses your innovative business ideas

Collaborate or Get Help

What do you do if you can't write good copy? Simple, get help. If your strengths don't lie in writing good copy, you really should get someone to lend a hand or certainly get them to read your entry once you've written it. Or you may want to collaborate with colleagues or partners and get them to enter for you. Note your thoughts and ideas, and when you have a first draft, get a friend or colleague to assist in drafting the final entry.

My Top Tip

You can also search www.dictionary.com and www.thesaurus.com to help you find strong active copy. Or take a peek at software such as WordWeb Pro (www.wordweb.info) which is a thesaurus that offers sentence ideas for words.

Dos

✓ Research the variety of business awards
✓ Copy the questions to your PC
✓ Think long and hard about the answers
✓ Highlight your USPs
✓ Show your industry expertise
✓ Prove to the judges that you're the best entry
✓ Understand what the award is all about
✓ Take the plunge and send in your best entry

Don'ts

✗ Don't try and impress with jargon and techie terms
✗ Don't ramble – judges won't tolerate rambling paragraphs with no focus
✗ Don't sit back and think you don't stand a chance and then leave it for another time. Take a risk, make the most of it and you may surprise yourself

Top Entry Tips

There are 1000s of business awards, and you can't enter them all, so take time to research them and decide which to enter.

1. *Research and do your homework*: Read all the details carefully and find out what the judges are looking for.

2. *Choose wisely*: Pick the awards that you have the best chance of winning.

3. *Enter to win*: Ensure you choose relevant and specific awards.

4. *Refine your entry*: Be open about your strengths and demonstrate this to the judges.

5. *Prove your claim*: You must be able to show why you are the best. Illustrate with graphs or market trends and even PR clippings.

6. *Good quality entries impress judges*: Plan your answers and answer every question. Once your entry is complete, mull it over for a few days before submission – go back to it a few times with new thoughts and inspiration.

7. *Some entries require you to be nominated*: Ask a valued friend or colleague to enter on your behalf.

8. *If necessary, hold off* until the following year to strengthen your chances of being a finalist.

9. *Impress judges* by writing in clear, simple yet professional business language and preferably in the third person.

Above all, try to demonstrate a 'Wow Factor'. This could be your client list, speed of growth, challenges you have overcome or simply your dynamism and over-the-top enthusiasm for your business concept.

Judging

Assessing what the judges are looking for in a winner is vital to your success. Put yourself in the judges' shoes and see your entry as they would. You may think your business is wonderful, but why would they? By looking at it from a new perspective you will present them with a champion entry. The judges need to set your entry apart from all the others. So, in order to stand out from the crowd, find creative ways to answer the questions. Many awards will want to know about your sales and business growth, ROI, competitors and even future expansion. Provide graphs and key performance indicators to strengthen your application if this is appropriate to this particular award.

Inject your passion and personality into your entry by highlighting any challenges, successes, inspiration and ambitions. Above all, you should be able to demonstrate why your product or service is the best thing since peanut butter. Show off your business success, even if it is only a micro or small business, shout it from the rooftops. The judge will hear!

Shout about It

Be positive and prepare to make the most of your win. If you're chosen as a finalist, be bold enough to write a press release about your award nomination and send it to the media. Local, regional, national and specialist industry publications will want to hear about your success. Wherever you can, get clients, customers and link partners to feature your story. Be proud to show off your award or nomination in all your marketing, on your website, and in communications with your customers and clients.

Frogs and Pancakes

Imagine winning a mentor who is one of the most successful woman entrepreneurs in the UK! I was awarded one of the best prizes – Karen Darby – as my mentor in the FreshIdeas Events Award. This screen-shot shows the moment I 'won' Karen.

We've had the greatest fun, from her flipping pancakes and serving them with ice cream at our meetings to fishing frogs out of her pond for an exhibition!

Aside from the good laughs, Karen has given me bucketloads of inspiration and her confidence in our business concept has been a huge boost. Every time I see her I walk away buzzing with excitement and with creative thoughts whirring in every direction. If you do nothing else today, enter some awards and find yourself a mentor!

PR Monitoring and Measurement

How will you know your PR plans have worked? In Day 9 we examined the excellent online tools to track, analyse and measure your social media campaigns. Do the same for each activity in the channels you choose. For example, if you are doing a PR campaign you can decide to pay for a PR monitoring service or you can track this via Google Alerts at no charge and keep a record of any press clippings.

As with social media monitoring, tracking and measuring your PR and media coverage is a vital part of your job as a 'pimp publicist'. Along with your reputation management, you will monitor targeted media to find out what things are being said about your site or business, whether this is good, bad or ugly. Measuring your publicity campaigns will establish if your key messages are getting picked up or are falling by the wayside.

 My Top Tip

Whether you monitor press coverage for sourcing media leads to contact, track your own coverage or simply gather industry intelligence, newspaper content offers a rich and valuable resource. However, do be aware that if you want to display or reuse any clippings you need to get permission from the publication or a license from the Newspaper Licensing Agency. They provide permission and access to newspaper content. Find out more from www.nla.co.uk. Lexis Nexis offer a similar service.

Media monitoring used to include newspapers, magazines, websites, radio and TV, but today it also includes the length and breadth of the web and social media world. In the good old days, it was a time-Hoover and expensive to boot. A publicist would read, check, analyse and collate publications or receive a pile of press clippings from a PR monitoring service. If you have the budget they are worth their salt. Basically, they have sophisticated systems in place which give you a summary and ROI so you can assess the return on investment for each clipping.

You can, of course, do this yourself by contacting the relevant outlet to see their column centimetre rate, which is the rate that they charge for advertising in their paper. You can work out what it would have cost you, had you advertised instead of getting free press coverage. In its simplest form this will give you a value for your PR clippings.

If you have already set up your Google Alerts for your social media, set one up for each press release you send out. As I mentioned before, you can also use Google Reader as a quick way to organise these alerts into a folder for easy analysis.

There may be services out there that offer complete monitoring of all offline and online PR and SM. However, these may be expensive so find a way to monitor and track your PR that suits your pocket and your diary.

Summary

Writing and submitting a press release is not about sales talk or advertising jargon. It is about news and the people behind the news. Today, we went behind the scenes and peeked into the minds of editors and journalists to see what ticks their boxes. Understanding how a reporter or editor wants to receive news is important in order to prevent your press releases gathering dust in a news desk bin or, even worse, buried under an editor's old teabag or banana skin!

If you optimise your press releases you will also bring traffic to your site. These good-quality links will also help to increase your Page Rank. Finding human interest stories will attract the media and give you a personal touch because visitors feel they know you by the time they get to check out your site.

Today we also explored all the cool and fab tools available for start-ups and business owners intent on tackling their own PR. It can be expensive, so weigh up the best products and services for your PR strategy. Don't forget to ask for a free trial each time to access the full potential the software can provide. A good idea is to consider sharing these PR tools with another business. Or sign up to iHubbub's Home Business Publicity Club (ihubbub.com/publicity-club).

I am sure by now you realise that there are so many PR tools at your fingertips. Winning an award is another way to gain recognition for all your hard work and it will certainly bring credibility to your business venture. Take a stab at it and have fun. Most of all, relish the moment when you win!

Day 12
Email Marketing

Today you will learn:

- ■ The benefits of email marketing
- ■ How to set up an email template
- ■ Why great subject lines are vital
- ■ How to set up an email campaign

Email marketing is probably the most effective digital method of marketing your online business because it is fast, cost-effective, personalised, flexible and, above all, targeted. Essentially, email marketing is a course of action you undertake to deliver your marketing messages about your product or service to a group of people or recipients who have opted into your email mailing list. This is done through electronic mail with a relevant, engaging and timely enewsletter, eshot or emailing campaign.

Why Email Marketing?

As with all your marketing efforts, your email marketing starting point has to be your visitors' interest in your product or service. Email marketing works a treat when run alongside your PR and marketing campaigns. It substantiates your brand and up-weights your key messages – even more so if they are designed and written for your target audience. Of course, it goes without saying that you must ensure your brand stands up to its promise in all your email marketing campaigns.

It is imperative that you have permission to email your recipients, that they have opted in or that you already have an 'email relationship' with them.

To get you started, go back and take a peek at your digital marketing objectives in Day 1. Now look at your PR and marketing from the previous chapters and then think about the reasons why you want to use email marketing and, more importantly, how it will benefit your website.

You need to set goals for your email marketing, which may include some of the following:

- Sell products or services
- Communicate and build rapport
- Announce special offers
- Entertain, inform and enlighten
- Add value to your brand
- Advance new client leads and develop current clients

The Email Marketing Process

1. *Set-up and Implementation:* Here you will think about why you want to start email marketing, what messages you will send out and how you will do this.

2. *Data Collection:* You'll need to start building a mailing list, which is best done organically. Remember that eBooks and Webinars are a great way to build a database list.

3. *Template Design:* Depending on your B2B or B2C audience, you can search email providers' template designs and then tweak to suit your site.

4. *Send and Delivery:* Send yourself a test. And then test it again. Each time you make one little change, do another test. Also do a spam check to prevent your email being dumped into junk mail.

5. *Reporting and Analysis:* The great graphs and stats you get from your delivery reports will help you see where you went wrong or right with a campaign. For example, check if you have had lots of unsubscribes which means your message or copy didn't tick boxes. Forwards to friends show you were on the spot with your email content.

As before, we will put ourselves in our visitors' shoes and write content for their interests. They are the ones who will either follow your 'call-to-action' or delete your email and tell you to go away.

> *"Measure success in order to improve your future campaigns. If you're unsure go to a specialist ESP for delivery."*
>
> Anthony Quigley, WebKitchen

With this in mind, go back to your notes about why you should put yourself in their shoes and remind yourself how they think and feel. Hopefully, you won't need to keep going back to your notes as this should be ingrained in you by now!

"

Anthony Quigley on Email Marketing

Anthony gives some useful notes on the different types of email that can be used:

1. Short editorial: alerts, press releases, tip of the day and product launches
   - These messages are short and to the point
   - They inform your subscribers about news and tips
   - This is not a 'sales hammer' so the content should be focused on editorial rather than promotion. A suggested balance is around 70% editorial:30% promotion
2. Long editorial: email newsletters, long press releases and industry guides
   - Allows you to write a little bit more
   - Many companies choose to send long form editorial to customers and prospects
   - This is not a sales pitch
   - Use this space to promote offers and buying information
3. Short promotional: e-cards, sale announcements and reminders
   - Keep this type of email short and sweet
   - The aim is to get the reader off the email and onto your site as quickly as possible
   - Take one key message and promote it
   - Must have a clear benefit to the recipient
4. Long promotional: sales letter and catalogue email
   - Allows you to present many benefits of your product or service
   - Also allows you to present many products on one email
   - Ideal for products or services that require more explanation
   - Direct sales driven, so your copy should reflect this

"

My Top Copywriting Tips
- Target your message to the right audience
- Get to the point and keep it simple
- Give the recipient more than one link
- Provide relevant information
- Sign your work
- Make your email copy scannable
- 3-second comprehension
- Make sure your call-to-action is obvious
- Use a short and clear subject line

E-news

An excellent way to kick start a great working relationship with your visitors is to set up a regular e-newsletter. You may only have five people on your new list, but no-one knows that. Just by getting started, you look the business. As your list grows, your e-news will evolve and hopefully one day will become a revenue generator. Some e-newsletters exist solely to generate huge profits for some companies. The more targeted and niche your audience, the more in demand your list will become.

Using a Template Design

The exciting part of email marketing is that you don't have to rush out and get a designer to create an email template. It's all done for you by the various email software suppliers. Firstly though, you should set guidelines to maintain your brand.

Begin by having a wade through your inbox. Get out your muddy boots and step into your deleted and junk folders. Find all the emails you deleted and analyse why. Then delete them from your deleted box. Yuck, they're gone now.

Next, see if there are any emails you may have forwarded to a friend. Keep those for future reference as they surely should be half decent if you wanted to share it.

Lastly, remind yourself of the best e-newsletters you have signed up for and if you haven't, then go to a few of your favourite sites as well as your competitors' sites and sign up to receive their newsletters – you can always remove yourself after your homework is done.

Now look at all of these with new eyes. Email marketing eyes.

Email Design Dos
✓ Keep HTML emails to 500–600 pixels in width
✓ Always add 'View this email in a browser'
✓ Design your emails with a minimum of images
✓ Test your emails in different email clients, such as Outlook, Googlemail, Hotmail, etc
✓ Always use a valid and consistent reply address
✓ Personalise your template

Email Design Don'ts
✗ NEVER use attachments
✗ Beware of too many font styles in your emails; stick to your brand
✗ The use of flash and JavaScript in emails is not advised
✗ Don't design and send your email as one big image, as your recipient may get an empty email
✗ Never put vital information in an image format as it may not be immediately visible and therefore could be overlooked

Email Template Essentials

Here are some top tips and key components for ensuring your template is successful in getting your mailing list to respond favourably to your email marketing campaigns.

Subject Lines
Your subject line is probably the most important gear in your email marketing, because it determines whether or not your email will be opened, read or deleted.

Without a compelling subject line, all of your hard work, template design, content layout, special offers and pre-testing drops your campaign dead before it's even begun.

Ensure effective campaigns by testing and alternating different subject lines. Always aim to gain attention and stand out from the 'inbox' crowd with intriguing, short and snappy one liners. The whole idea of email communication is to drive traffic to your website, not to make them delete before reading past your subject line.

Overall Design
- Short, sharp, snappy subject line is essential
- Hook them and get them to read on
- Simple, clear, fresh, easy-to-read layout
- Don't clutter with too many articles
- Design for plain text, HTML and blocked images
- Recognition of your brand encourages opening the email
- Brand your website's name by using this in the 'From' email address, which also enforces trust and reinforces your brand's value
- Keywords and messages 'above the fold', in other words, above the computer screen's cut-off point
- Plan your template with a specific reader in mind – they all need a different approach and content

Layout
- Primary message on top left, visible in preview
- Mirror your website header and footer to add value to your brand
- Be consistent with fonts and colours, stick to your brand's image
- Secondary message on top right
- Boxes can also highlight or pull out certain sections or key points

Content
- Be friendly and welcoming
- Use active power words
- Less is more, simple, short and sweet is best
- Sign up or special offer should be upfront

- Subhead primary article
- Summarise key message in first sentence
- Include links back to your site in every article
- Remember people scan-read so get to the point quickly
- Divide up long pieces with bullets or numbers
- Like your content, use subheaders to draw in the eye
- Use corporate business language for B2B
- Chatty, conversational and personable tone for B2C

Email Extras to Add to Your Template

To keep up your viral marketing place a 'Forward to a friend' link way up front and have your social media links clearly visible. Use your company tagline or slogan, preferably at the top so the reader can instantly recognise and 'trust' the email. You may want to ask them to add you to their safe senders' list. I use a 'view in browser' link in case the recipient prefers to read your email in an online version instead of in email format. Remember your golden SEO rules and include alt tags on all your images and avoid 'click here', instead use keywords as links. Highlight your call-to-action upfront and repeat it a few times throughout the email to strengthen the key message.

You could try inserting a table of contents to highlight 'what's in this month's e-news' to tease the reader to continue reading. Add a printer-friendly button, especially if your product or service reflects an environmentally-friendly concept. Don't forget to add links to advertisers or sponsors of the newsletter. Always have an unsubscribe option; all providers should have this automated, which means you don't even see it, but it is there, you'll see it in your tests. Ensure your unsubscribe link works by sending yourself an email and testing it.

Testing Your Emails

What you have to do next can be fun, but it can also be tedious. You need to check your little stash of emails from above in a variety of ways and make notes on the outcomes.

First up, see what they look like in Outlook, then if you have a Gmail or Hotmail account, send it to yourself or some friends. Ask them to take a screenshot and send it back to you or, when it arrives, get them to ask you over for coffee.

You now have a choice:

1. Assess the email in a preview panel in Outlook.

2. Or you can simply ensure that your email provider does this preview testing for you.

Many ISPs will block images so make a note of who sends plain text emails or HTML emails. Also note whether their images are blocked.

My Top Tip

Be sure to use an alt tag on images in your template. It works well to inform email recipients viewing a blocked image marked with an x what the image is all about. This should encourage them to download the image and thus see the full email.

What if you send out emails without testing, testing and testing again? Remember, if you hate receiving these kinds of emails yourself, imagine what your new visitors might think to see the same or similar results from you! You could risk wasted time and money.

Summary

Today we discovered why email marketing is the most effective digital method of marketing your online business. We also learnt how to ensure a fast, cost-effective, personalised and targeted campaign. We chatted about the top tips for ensuring a fab-looking template and discussed various options to ensure your email gets read and action is taken.

The key points to always keep in mind: collect 'opt ins' to ensure the best list and all your emails should be relevant to each recipient. Always conform to the legalities, clean your list regularly and send inspiring emails with great subject lines and 'calls-to-action'.

If you don't have time to do all this yourself, search for 'email marketing agencies' or 'email marketing designers' and see the vast choice on the Google platter. Email marketing solution providers have hundreds of templates just waiting for you to pounce on and which are designed to avoid these issues. We will now move on and set up an Email Marketing Toolkit of lists and software suppliers, and get to understand more about email delivery.

Day 13
Email Marketing Tools

Today you will learn:

■ How to ensure legal compliance

■ The most effective ways to build a mailing list

■ Which email solution providers to use

■ How to be aware of and check for spam

Email Marketing Solution Providers

The advantages of using an email marketing solution is that most suppliers will give you a free trial to suss it out before you sign up for a subscription. They have a WYSIWYG editor to make email marketing life easier with a smorgasbord of designer templates so you don't have to start from scratch. They also offer stats dynamically generated in handy graphs for you to monitor and track the results of your campaigns. If this all seems a bit too much too soon, most of them do offer training, but this may be chargeable.

Email marketing can become extremely costly so compare rates as annual costs can be higher than monthly charges. Also, if you're new to this form of digital marketing, find out if they have a support team and consider your country location. For example, can you get phone support in your business hours?

Before choosing whether to use one of these providers, decide what you need, whether it is cheap and cheerful or advanced and technical, and research the various suppliers and their templates before you approach them with your email marketing goals.

I suggest you give free trials a go, have a play with their templates, try sending emails by forming a small group of close family or friends and asking their forgiveness in advance. When they know what you're trialling they should understand. Be sure to ask for their feedback!

Here are a few suggested suppliers to start with, but do search for more as the scope ranges from a small spend, up to extremely sophisticated systems:

UK

GraphicMail: www.graphicmail.co.uk

GetResponse: www.getresponse.com

US

MailChimp: www.mailchimp.com

AWeber: www.aweber.com

SimplyCast: www.simplycast.com

Infacta: www.infacta.com

FreeAutobot: www.freeautobot.com

Constant Contact: www.constantcontacts.com

If you implement a contact relationship management (CRM) system into a Drupal site such as CiviCRM, they also offer a full emailing solution. I felt like a nerd in a geekie shop when I realised the power that this web-based CRM system offered as open source.

 CRM: A customer relationship management system, such as CiviCRM, allows an organisation to record and manage information about the various people and other organisations it deals with.

CiviCRM is more than just a contacts address book. It gives you the power to track interactions with your visitors and community members on your website. Although CiviCRM focuses on the needs of non-profits, it is also a great tool for small businesses. While most CRMs are focused on managing commerce, the beauty about CiviCRM is that it tracks revenue and income but also emphasises communication with individuals and

 OPEN SOURCE: Open Source means there are no license costs or user fees associated with downloading, installing or using the software.

community engagement, as well as managing emailing campaigns to your members. Take a look at www.civicrm.org<http://www.civicrm.org>.

Email Jargon

You are likely to come across a lot of technical terms when dealing with your email marketing. Here are some of the key ones.

Delivery is measured and monitored by the email marketing solution provider. Use their stats to monitor the effectiveness of your email being delivered to your mailing list.

Open rates can be used to test the effectiveness of emails, but they can be misleading. This is because some people view the email in their preview pane and may not actually click inside the body of the email to open it. This counts as an open, even if they don't read it.

A **click through rate** is when someone has clicked the links in your email and read the details on your website. Use click throughs to drive traffic back to your site with a good spread of keyword-rich hyperlinks.

A **conversion** is a successful sale of a product or service. It could also be a different goal such as membership registration, sign-up for an event or even sign-up to another newsletter. Test your conversions against the objectives or purpose of your email.

A **forward** is when you encourage someone to forward your email to family, friends and colleagues (F2F). You can do this with offers and competitions as you would do in a loyalty campaign. However, it is best achieved 'organically' by simply giving them great content that compels them to share and pass on to others. This is an ideal viral tool and, if done correctly, can create an incredible buzz with an F2F campaign.

Testing, Testing 1,2,3

When you think you're ready, you're not. You must send the email to yourself and others to test and test it again. There are thousands of dodgy 'work-from-home schemes' and this has made it harder for our legitimate and genuine work-from-home jobs to get through spam radars.

Anthony Quigley's Guide to Email Testing

Anthony has kindly given us the steps he uses when starting a new email campaign:

Identify:
- Customer actions (conversions)
- Brand affinity (opens)
- Content relevancy (click throughs)

Discover:
- Which offer is best for your overall customer base?
- Which groups of customers prefer specific offers? Learn as much as possible about your recipients.

Reporting:
- Testing increases ROI
- Small changes can make a big difference in results – subject line, sender name, offer placement
- Testers achieve 68% higher return over non-testers (Jupiter Research 2007)
- Note that most marketers don't test

Recommended Delivery Times:
- 80 percent of emails are opened between 5am and 5pm
- 62 percent are opened between Tuesday and Thursday
- Business customers are most likely to open during a working day
- Personal email accounts are often checked during the day
- Consider that the time to deliver is the time you want the traffic

Testing Loop

When you first start testing your email campaigns, it may be best to follow these steps to ensure you know what to test and how to measure the results. Your first step is to decide what to test. You will need to analyse previous campaigns and pinpoint areas with most room for improvement.

Next comes measuring success and this can be done by checking your Google Analytics to see an increase in website traffic. You can also gauge response to an offer, sales, rates for 'opened' emails and links clicked through to your site. All of this is only done if you have chosen the right testing methodology. **A/B testing** is simple to set up and you take a section of data and test two different messages or subject lines with a handful of recipients. The one with the most opens and clicks to your site will give you the best result.

Lastly, test to compare and pick a winner. Send the winning version after 24 to 48 hours. This way you can implement this new data knowledge into your next campaign. However, do make sure you are comparing apples with apples.

Anthony's Hot Tip

Make sure you can attribute an increase or decrease in the area you measure directly to the email you send.

- Test subject lines for each campaign
- Use a control group to test frequency
- Take best practices with a grain of salt, test everything
- Track, document and share your testing results
- A lift in open rates should translate into more clicks and more conversions
- Today's test results may no longer be valid in 3 months

Your Checklist for Testing Emails

Checks to Perform on Every Email
- Spelling and grammar
- Top tips in order of priority
- Images tagged and viewable
- Check 'preview' and 'above the fold'
- Call-to-action must be prominent
- Download speed – fast or slow
- Hyperlinks and landing page links working
- Spam filters
- Legal compliance
- How does it look in different ISP clients: Gmail, Hotmail, Yahoo, AOL, Lotus, Outlook

Checks to Perform before Sending Email
- Test delivery in various ISPs to ensure your email isn't 'chewed up' or arrives as a blank email
- Anti-spam your content – most providers supply this. If not, test email with a spam checker: www.lyris.com/resources/contentchecker
- Silly things like Essex or West Sussex can play havoc with words like 'sex'

Checks to Perform after Sending Email
- Remove email addresses that bounce after 3 times
- Track opens, click throughs
- Monitor performance against other emails
- Analyse which links were clicked most

Bouncy Emails

Despite your checks, your email marketing can still bounce. A hard bounce is out of your control, and could be due to a number of different things:

- Blocked as spam
- Message too large

- Invalid domain
- Email address no longer exists

A soft bounce is when the email is trying to get through, but the server could be down, the person's mailbox is full or there is some other technical hitch.

Performance MOT

Like your car, your email marketing deserves a monthly, quarterly, periodic or annual check. Examining your stats can and should improve your email campaign performance. Try keeping a spreadsheet of all the emails you send, which will help you analyse your email marketing over a short- and long-term period. This can only improve its effectiveness. It will also reward your 'elbow grease' if you see high click throughs to landing pages and subsequent orders.

Items to Monitor
- Date sent
- Day sent
- Time sent
- Subject line
- Key messages
- Call-to-action
- Open rate
- Click through
- Landing links
- Unsubscribe number
- Which mailing list
- Bounces – hard and soft
- Sales, conversions or sign-ups

Spam and Deliver

You may have a pretty new design and your own niche data list, but neither of them are any good without a resolution for handling bounces. Like the bounce rate in

Google Traffic Analytics, an email bounce rate is when an email bounces and doesn't get through to the intended recipient for one reason or another. You may not be a plumber, but there are steps you can take to prevent blockages. See the definition of spam at www.spamhaus.org/definition.html.

Spam filters look for:

- Phrases
- Coding
- Header structure
- Phishing
- Image and text balance
- Reputation

You can either trawl through a painfully long list of what spam words to watch out for, or ensure that your email provider has this service built in. Google 'list of spam words' to find the worst spam words – avoid them like the plague!

Roadblocks

ISPs block spam. Take the following steps to ensure you avoid any words that could be seen as spam:

- Don't use misleading subject lines and headers
- Don't ask for money
- Don't mention 'Free' – this is a big spam no-no
- Don't use a strange 'From' email
- Don't promise the earth
- Don't give away 'top secrets'
- Don't promise to make someone rich overnight
- Don't promise to double someone's income
- Don't offer 'Hot tips' – another no-no
- Don't use a 'Do Not Reply' email, it puts people off and may encourage spam blockage

My Top Tip

Email marketers can check whether their IP address has been blacklisted by checking on Spamhaus. Take a look at their guidelines on spam, read their white papers and ensure you don't send junk mail: www.spamhaus.org/faq/answers.lasso?section= marketing%20faqs

'Do Not Reply'

I am constantly amazed by how many companies use a 'Do Not Reply' email address. What's the point of communicating with your audience if you tell them in no uncertain terms that you do not want them to reply! If you are trying to encourage and grow relationships with your audience you want an open two-way communication channel. Sending anything from a 'Do Not Reply' address indicates that you do not want to talk to them or hear their feedback. What a negative way to do business!

In my opinion, a better option is to use a business email address. We always use Ken, Paula or one of our team. This tells anyone who reads the email, even if it has been forwarded, that we are approachable. If you absolutely cannot use a personal email, make up a name and get someone to monitor that email account. At least that way you won't be using info, admin or enquiries as another generic put off.

OPT-IN EMAIL: This is when a visitor stumbles upon an option to receive an e-mail from a website. Normally, this is in the form of a 'bulk' email which means it is sent to loads of recipients at the same time. Opt ins work to help build a mailing list and is imperative for 'permission based email marketing' in order to prevent your message becoming spam.

Permission Impossible

Email marketers must bone up on permission practices before embarking on their first campaigns. Put yourself in your users' shoes one more time by imagining you were contacted constantly without your permission. Have you had that happen to you? Annoying, isn't it? Now that you're building your own mailing list, you want subscribing recipients to give permission. Failing to comply is a dangerous mission. Remember, only email people who have given permission to converse with you by email.

Building Your Mailing List

You need to start thinking about how to build a mailing list. This is best done organically, which means gathering data over time. The best way to build a data list is to set up an 'Opt In' list on your website. This is easily done through a mailing list. You can also run promotions and competitions as well as webinars.

Of course, if you have a community or membership site, such as iHubbub, this is a way of collating a list, but do be sure to have an unsubscribe button or link clearly visible if the members don't want to receive information from you. Better still – give them a selection so they can choose what they want to receive from your site and they can subscribe or unsubscribe at any time.

When someone does give you their email it is polite to show your appreciation with a thank-you page immediately after they have supplied their details.

Give your visitors something free to encourage them to join your mailing list. For example, I gave a free chapter of my first book to give readers a 'taste' for the book and to build a mailing list at the same time. You can offer any incentive, such as discounts, free delivery, link to white papers or reports or download a new eBook. Provide links for new visitors to sign up and receive your newsletters or ensure you have a tick box for this on your registration page. You can also do this when someone places an order or gets in touch via your contact page. Also consider doing joint promotions or joint ventures with relevant sites where you can both promote each other's product or service.

Email collection is not only restricted to online incentives. The most obvious way to collect emails is with telephone sales, feedback forms and by getting your receptionist to ask for this information. Whenever we run an event, we always find ways to build our list. I do the same for my training workshops and offer an incentive to encourage new names for my mailing list. This can be done quite simply on an A4 letterhead divided into three or four and cut into compliments-size slips of paper. For starters, you only need a space for an email address, first name and last name. You may also want to show email preference with an HTML or text box and possibly a phone number field if you intend to contact them.

My Top Tip

You may come across rented lists, which are ready-made targeted lists to help you get going quickly – but these can be very costly. However, the impersonal nature of these 'cold-calling' emails are far outweighed by the benefits of building your own members' list. Get started straight away and before you know it, you will have a budding mailing list on the boil.

Ideas for Building a List

Here are a few ways to build a relevant email database:

- Opt-in form on your contact page
- Face-to-face data collection
- Viral database building, such as 'forward to a friend'
- Web sign-up form, which must be easy to use, easy to find, non-intrusive and offer benefits
- EBook campaigns – ask for contact details in return for an eBook download
- Give advice tips or handy hints as an industry expert in a YouTube video in return for registration to a course
- Subscription or membership to your site

> ## Anthony Quigley on Data Cleansing
>
> - If you haven't cleaned it today, it's out of date
> - Every time you send you should clean
> - Focus on quality not quantity
> - Keep a full, clean data list
> - Group or segment it in some way
> - Lose the bad data even if they're customers
> - Bad data such as bounces need to be corrected or deleted

Segmentation

If you're just starting to collect and use data, now is the best time to consider segmenting your data lists. Doing this later on, when you have a large database, can be a pain and a mammoth task, and you will end up with untidy segments.

The first step is to decide what 'fields' you want to include in targeted segmentation. If you're familiar with 'mail merges' this will be old hat to you. Create a spreadsheet where each column is a data field such as first name, last name, company, address or town, county and country. You can also add a column for 'how heard' in order to monitor and track how your data list was made up and then segment names by marketing campaigns targets.

This can also be done in CiviCRM. For example, think of your immediate group of friends, connections and colleagues. In your mind, place them all in a room. Now go through each one by their first name, last name, town they live in and their favourite eats or drinks. Then, remember how or where you met them – this would be your 'how heard'.

Can you see how this starts to form a grouping picture in your mind of your closest friends? This should be done with your data, which can be segmented according to demographics, geography, history, relationships, life cycle, marketing campaigns, products bought, service types, behaviour and anything that is suitable to your site.

Legal Compliance

By ensuring you stick to the legal compliance acts, you will build confidence and credibility with your visitors as well as create trust. There are now relevant laws governing email marketing.

The Data Protection Act gives your customers the right to know what information is held about them, and sets out rules to make sure that you handle this information properly. Clear, concise details on your Data Protection practices will reinforce your customer relationships and foster an environment of trust when you email them. It is also a legal requirement as all organisations must make sure that they comply with the Data Protection Act. It requires all organisations that handle personal information to comply with eight important principles regarding privacy and disclosure.

Anyone who processes personal information must make sure that their customer's personal information is:

- Secure
- Fairly and lawfully processed
- Processed for limited purposes
- Adequate, relevant and not excessive
- Accurate and up to date
- Not kept for longer than is necessary
- Processed in line with your rights

Read more details on the following compliance laws:

- BNA: Business Names Act 1985 (Companies Act)
- DDA: Disability and Discrimination Act 1999
- DPA: Data Protection Act 1998
- ECD: Electronic Commerce Regulations 2002 (EC Directive)
- PECR: Privacy and Electronic Communications Regulations 2003

The Institute of Direct Marketing offers advice on permission based practises and rules. The best route to go with all of your email marketing campaigns, stick to the

Data Protection Act. Look it up, read it, get it stuck in your mind or branded on your brain. Full stop.

Summary

Building your own members' list is the most valuable way to leverage your brand because you have created a relationship with the recipient of your emails. Get up to speed on the jargon so you are familiar with all the terminology and email marketing becomes second nature to you. Discover new ways in your business to build an organic emailing list, but you can easily start with offers and incentives.

Research all the legalities to ensure your emails comply with email marketing laws. You have found that the best way to build data is organically with a good mailing list. Be sure you test and test again, as things often can and do go pear-shaped even on test runs. You also learnt that spam filters can be tough on your email campaigns so read through all the spam words. Even better – use a spam checker if your email provider has one on offer. This will help to prevent your email being trashed before your recipient gets a glimpse of it.

Day 14
The End of
the Beginning

Coming successfully to the end of this book means that you are now ready to start the journey to pimp your site. Your next steps are to keep reading and learning more about online marketing and PR in order to keep your site optimised, marketed and publicised. Of the Battle of Egypt, Winston Churchill said: "This is not the end. It is not even the beginning of the end. But it is, perhaps, the end of the beginning."

Getting this far in the book may be the end of your beginning and the start of your voyage of discovery and excitement of putting all these cool tools into practise. The more you work at your website to make it a success, the more excited and empowered you will become. Focus on what you have achieved so far and what you will achieve next. Think of it as having no end. Like the seed you plant in your garden, your site's DMS is constantly growing and will flourish with lots of TLC.

Here are some key points to maintain your ongoing success:

1. Always have a Positive Attitude

We are all blasted by bad news so why not offer something positive? Instead of distributing negative news through your social media channels, remind your community of followers of all the right reasons to be optimistic. Your help and encouragement as someone who has been through the same process will enrich their site. Talk openly about your failures and how you turned those 'lessons learnt' into achievements. They will admire you all the more for this. It only takes one small idea, gesture or step to help someone. Sharing mistakes you've made (remember the examples I've shared in this book) will also remind you to preserve that positive attitude on your own site's evolution. Spread hope.

2. Recognition of People around You

Recognise others around you who may be helping you with your digital marketing or working on your site and even contacts you have made through your networking connections. Showing appreciation for even the smallest achievement should come naturally to you. If not, become a giver. Whether you recognise and encourage people in public or private it stimulates them to do the same with those around them. And so the effect becomes viral. Grab the opportunity to lift them and help them grow – this may be personally or in business. Praising someone not only gives them a huge boost, but has this incredible magical effect of 'giving' back to you too. It's the way to go. To use my partner's phrase – it's the future!

3. Emulate Others

More than likely there are lots of people around you that you admire, look up to and want to emulate. They may be inspiring, knowledgeable or just downright feisty about making their business a success. Whatever it is about them that lights your fire, imitate their best qualities in order to make an impact on your own business life.

4. Be Emulated

Go one further. You are a fantastic example to others. You may not think this or know it, but you are. The knowledge you have and the experiences you have encountered are worth following. Your passion, energy and interest in others will prove you care and draw people to you. How cool will it be if one of your networking fans or followers tells you that they *so* want to be like you and do the things you do?

5. Express Yourself

Your social media influence will shoot up when you express your excitement and passion for your subject of interest. And the cherry on top – it's contagious. There is a lovely Irish saying: 'Smile, it makes people wonder what you've been up to.' It's not only true, but it deepens your experience by either stirring other people emotionally at seeing your joy or spurring them into action to do something for themselves.

6. Exude Passion and Energy

I believe that passion and energy equals success. After the Remote Worker Awards Ceremony, Ken and I were inundated with finalists telling us how thrilled they were to be included in the Awards, even if they had not won. It set some people off on a mission to enter more awards, which they have gone on to win. It is delightful to see their determination to be successful and all because something we did spurred them on. In turn, we were so inspired by all of these people in the same boat as us and we wanted to do whatever we could to help them. All these freelancers and home workers networking created a real 'hubbub'. There is something so special about the energy and passion the home working revolution generates. The very essence of this 'excited fuss' is the inspiration behind iHubbub. Thus the idea for iHubbub.com was born. It grew out of wanting to share our knowledge and broaden the horizons for the home working community.

7. Inspire Others

Different things inspire different people. Some feel a sense of camaraderie at being in the same shoes and being challenged by the same situations as other people. Sharing what these are and how you have overcome them may encourage someone to rush out and tackle their own struggle head on. Others may be moved by your determination and way of turning negatives to positives. No matter what or how, inspiration brings people together in unusual ways. So draw on your skills and expertise to inspire people in your network, even if it is only helping and guiding them in whatever sector you specialise. Seize even the smallest notch to instil confidence, infuse motivation and generally stimulate people around you – it's a huge buzz!

8. Keep the Inspirational Juice Flowing

At the same time that you are inspiring others, be inspired by other websites and their trends, by people you meet and work with and by new innovations on the market. Listen to people talking and ask questions about anything that sparks your attention. Keep thinking laterally and even insist on a monthly brainstorm with your management team, even if it is only two of you! And if you're on your own, brainstorm with yourself! Why not? It will keep your inspirational juices flowing and this fluid is often the lifeblood of a new site.

9. Show Magnetic Force

Just like a new flower attracts bees, a fresh and exciting site attracts customers, clients and the media. Think of your favourite flower and then plant your face into its beauty. Now imagine lots of bees and butterflies all wanting a taste of your nectar. Give it freely because the *more* you share, the *more* they'll come back for *more*. By this, I mean communicate your experiences, share your generosity, reveal your personality and demonstrate your talents. Having an exceptional service or stunning product range will add to the excitement of knowing you and being around you. As your magnetic force grows in stature, so does your business and your bottom line. Let's put a spin on that fantastic saying: "Does my bottom look big in this?" Let's say it this way: "Does my bottom-line look *big enough* in this?" So, believe in yourself and in your own ability, and people will be attracted to you and engage with your site's offering.

10. Visualise Your Goals

Whatever it is you want to do with your site, you need to aspire to a level in order to achieve it. Recognising your aspirations and actually visualising them will lead to achievement and result in success. Use imagery to stimulate your thought processes. Picture where you want to go and what you want to do with your website. In tough times, recall this image and renew your determination to make it work. Forget the fact that you couldn't afford to get a PR resource to promote your business or you didn't have development funding to set up a new area of your site.

Instead, remember the risks you have taken and all the things you have given up to get this far. This alone should shove you along to the next determined stepping stone.

But don't stop there, keep that image – of how your site will one day look or how much traffic it will receive or even how popular you will become in the media – in the front of your mind. When I first met Karen Darby she told me how she fixed an image of her dream house in her mind and was delighted when she sold her business for many millions and went out to buy that same house. Karen would love it if you copied her and focus on what you want 'real bad'.

A business or personal visual target is the best way to get you through all the daily juggling. Don't just stick this image on your fridge, pin it up on your frontal brain lobes. The best way to get somewhere is to want it badly enough!

11. Become a BIG Thinker

Aim high. It's as simple as that. So what if you've only just started a website or if you're a small player. Discuss your plans to grow and give your customers and clients examples of your competitive edge. You will reap bigger rewards if you aim for the sky. So when you plan your goals think BIG and believe you can achieve whatever you set out to do. Keep this book in your bag or briefcase. I use a Dictaphone and take a notebook everywhere I go and as inspiration floats by, I grab it.

Being constantly inspired and motivated by others around you will fuel your desire to reach for your dreams and achieve your goals. It will work wonders if you inject your natural enthusiasm into what you do best. We should all dream – I certainly do. I visualise our site traffic and getting loads of members. I can even see actual members in my mind's eye. This helps to ground your aims into real situations and, more importantly, into real people.

Pluck the name of any online millionaire or business entrepreneur out of thin air and know that they were once in your shoes. They went through all that you are going through and because they were BIG thinkers, they achieved their dreams.

Don't be afraid to be a dreamer and don't underestimate the power of dreaming. Don't be distracted by competitors, challenges, downfalls or risks. Instead, keep your eyes and heart focused on the ultimate outcome of your digital plans. It can be a long and rocky road building up site traffic and business awareness.

Hopefully, this book has given you tons of inspiration and motivated you to brainstorm new ideas and learn new skills to prepare you for the ongoing digital marketing journey ahead. It would also be lovely to know that it has encouraged you to become a lifelong learner. You'll achieve more in life if you keep learning new skills, be it personal or business.

Being enthusiastic, inspired, motivated and eager to inspire others is powerful. Don't just dream. Dream big dreams.

Summary

Before you dart off to follow your dreams, I want to remind you of the key points listed in this book. Here is a list of the key factors to Pimp Your Site:

1. Decide on your primary keywords to use in On Page SEO.

2. Use SEO Tools to ensure you get all the right keywords.

3. Ensure all the right metadata is in place.

4. Start a link-building campaign to create back links.

5. Sign up for Twitter, Facebook, iHubbub and LinkedIn to become a practised user.

6. Plan your marketing and PR campaign activities and analyse their success.

7. Write effective press releases and a dynamic PR strategy.

8. Try various PR tools and media alerts.

9. Use eMarketing tools to connect with your audience.

10. Keep teaching yourself new ways to Pimp Your Site!

When you get through this list, congratulate yourself and give yourself a great reward. If you enjoyed this journey with me, you may want to take part in one of my training course workshops. Have a look at iHubbub (www.ihubbub.com) and think about joining to promote, market and publicise your website or home business. You will also be able to connect with our experts and find all the latest options to 'Pimp Your Site'. If you are an expert in your industry sector we would love to hear from you. You could do a training webinar for our members to show off your skills and be featured in our expert's panel. We promote our experts to the media so you can't go wrong. If you have any questions or if you want to share your story with me, please feel free to make contact via my site or iHubbub's contact page.

Thank you for reading this book. I hope you have enjoyed reading it as much as I enjoyed writing it!

Jargon Buster

AD RANK: This is one of the means Google uses to determine an advert's ranking on the Search Results pages. The formula is a multiplication: the maximum amount you're prepared to pay per click multiplied by the actual Click Through Rate % your ad is receiving. CPC × CTR = Ad Rank Score.

ABSOLUTE UNIQUE VISITOR: Number of distinct devices (PCs) active on the site over the reporting period.

AVG. CPC: The average cost per click for a campaign. This is calculated as the amount spent divided by the number of clicks received.

BOUNCE RATE: Analytics track these bounces to inform you how many visitors you are losing.

CACHE: A computer component that stores data transparently so that it can be retrieved quickly later on. It allows Google to store each word in every page it finds.

CRM (Customer Relationship Management system): This allows an organisation to record and manage information about the various people and other organisations it deals with.

CTR (%): The Click Through Rate for a campaign. This is calculated as the number of clicks received divided by the number of impressions.

CONVERSION: User achieves a defined goal. This helps you to see how good your site is at turning traffic into goals such as signing up for an event or registering on the site or paying for an item. It gives you the ability to gauge how hard your site is working.

GOOGLE ANALYTICS: This is the easiest way to track your traffic and analyse your website stats.

HTML: Hypertext markup language – the code used to write web pages.

IMPRESSION: The number of times the ads in a campaign have been shown to users.

INDEX: Content and source code is analysed and indexed according to the titles, headings or meta tags you have used.

KEI: The Keyword Effectiveness Index is used when testing your keywords and their effectiveness.

KPIs (Key Performance Indicators): Identifies and quantifies key areas of your website as the best or worst performers. This information will show you how well your site is performing and where to focus your energy.

METADATA: Data about your web pages which can be added into the background of your site through your admin section.

MICROSITE: A single web page or a few pages acting as an 'accessory' to a website. They can be used to add special information on a given topic or for promotional purposes such as extended details on events or editorial articles.

OPEN SOURCE: Open Source means there are no license costs or user fees associated with downloading, installing or using the software.

OPT-IN EMAIL: This is when a visitor stumbles upon an option to receive an e-mail from a website. Opt-ins work to help build a mailing list and is imperative for 'permission based email marketing' in order to prevent your message becoming spam.

ORGANIC SEARCH: This is always on the left-hand side and reflects Google's ranking in importance to relevant keywords.

PAGE IMPRESSION: A page is (re)loaded by a user, a measure of volume.

PAY PER CLICK: Pay Per Click marketing is the most measurable and effective form of marketing ever designed by human beings. As suggested by the name, you only Pay each time someone Clicks on your advert, so you should be attracting people who are already interested in what you have to offer.

QUALITY SCORE: This is Google's definition of how relevant your advert, and its destination URL, are for a particular search query.

ROI (Return On Investment): A term to measure PR and Marketing performance in order to establish which campaigns work best and why.

RSS: Real Simple Syndication is clever technology to allow you to subscribe to a website's content by a feed.

RSS READER: The application to monitor your selected feeds.

SEO : Search Engine Optimisation is the process of improving ranking in search engine results.

SM: Social media is a group of easy-to-use web-based systems that allow you to engage with a group of followers or fans.

SOCIAL STREAM: A wave of content that populates your various social sites.

SPONSORED LINKS: These are found on the right-hand side and sometimes on top of the left side of a search result. Companies pay to be featured on Google Adwords.

UNIQUE VISITOR: A unique visitor is a person who has visited your website at least once in a fixed time period, which can be per day, per week or per month. This term is used in web stats to count each visitor to your website once in the time frame of the analytics report. If they visit your site seven times a day they will only be counted as one unique visitor for that day or week or month. This stat is used to measure your site's true audience or 'reach'.

URL: Each page on your website will have its own URL (Universal Resource Locator), normally generated from the page title and should have an individual 'address' for each of your web pages.

VISIT: Stream of activity by a unique visitor.

VLOGS: A form of blogging via video. A vlog or video blog is a form of internet TV and is sometimes combined with text blogging and video.

WIDGET: A cool gadget that can be set up in various online platforms to create nifty tools to insert HTML code into your site.

WYSIWYG: What You See Is What You Get application for creating and editing websites.

XML: Code readable by search engines.

Useful Resources

Digital Marketing

Bing: www.bing.com

Enquiro: www.enquiro.com/enquiro-develops-googles-golden-triangle.php

Google: www.google.com

URL example: www.remoteemployment.com/news

Yahoo!: www.yahoo.com

Keyword Tools

Google search queries: adwords.google.co.uk/select/KeywordToolExternal

Google: www.google.com/sktool

www.keywordspy.co.uk

www.spyfu.com

www.traffictravis.com

www.wordtracker.com

Search Engine Marketing

Web Directories

Business.com: www.business.com

dmoz: www.dmoz.org and www.dmoz.com

GoGuides: http://www.goguides.org

Joeant: http://www.joeant.com

Yahoo!: http://dir.yahoo.com

Local and Regional Directories

FreeIndex: www.freeindex.co.uk

Kyotee: www.kyotee.co.uk

Parent Pages: www.parentpages.co.uk

Streets Local: www.streetslocal.co.uk

TheiGroup: www.theigroup.co.uk

Thomsonlocal.com: www.thomsonlocal.com

UK Classifieds: www.ukclassifieds.co.uk

Yell: www.yell.com

SEO

Influence Finder: www.influencefinder.com

Scribe SEO: www.scribeseo.com

SEO Book: www.seobook.com

SEOMoz: www.seomoz.org

SEO PowerSuite: www.seo-powersuite.com

Adwords

Facebook: www.facebook.com/adsmarketing

Google: http://adwords.google.co.uk

Internet Advertising Bureau (IAB): www.iab.net

Online Marketing

Share Buttons

AddThis: www.addthis.com

Delicious: www.delicious.com

Digg: www.digg.com

Gigya: www.gigya.com

reddit: http://www.reddit.com/

ShareThis: www.sharethis.com

SocialFollow: www.socialfollow.com

SocialTwist: www.socialtwist.com

StumbleUpon: www.stumbleupon.com

Blogging

Blog Grader: www.blog.grader.com

Blog Pulse: www.blogpulse.com

Blogger Linkup: www.bloggerlinkup.com

Bloglines: www.bloglines.com

Hubspot: www.hubspot.com and www.hubspot.com/blogging-kit

My Blog Guest: www.myblogguest.com

ProBlogger: www.probloggerbook.com and www.problogger.net

Submit Your Article: www.submityourarticle.com

Technorati: www.technorati.com

Windows Live Writer: http://explore.live.com/windows-live-writer

Article Distribution Channels

Amazines: www.amazines.com

Article Alley: www.articlealley.com

ArticleCity: www.articlecity.com

Articlegold: www.articlegold.com

Buzzle: www.buzzle.com

EzineArticles: www.ezinearticles.com

GoArticles: www.goarticles.com

Submit Your Article: www.submityourarticle.com

eBook

eBook Design: www.serif.com/pageplus

eBook Reader: www.nextup.com/TextAloud

eMag Creator: www.emagcreator.com

iHubbub eBooks: www.iHubbub.com/eBooks

Scribd: www.scribd.com

Smashwords: www.smashwords.com

Video

Blip.tv: www.blip.tv

Brightcove: www.brightcove.com

Camtasia: www.techsmith.com/camtasia.asp

ClipShack: www.clipshack.com

Crackle: www.crackle.com

Dailymotion: www.dailymotion.com

Flip Video: www.flipvideo.co.uk

Podcast.com: www.podcast.com

Screencast: www.Screencast.com

Spike: www.spike.com

TechCrunch: www.Techcrunch.com

Twitvid: www.Twitvid.com

Viddler: www.viddler.com

Vimeo: www.vimeo.com

Windows Live Movie Maker: http://explore.live.com/windows-live-movie-maker

Yahoo! Video: www.video.yahoo.com

YouTube Insights: www.youtube.com

Social Media

Acquia: www.acquia.com

Facebook Fanpage: www.facebook.com/pages/create.php or www.facebook.com/pages/learn.php

Facebook Plugins and Like Button: http://developers.facebook.com/docs/reference/plugins/like

Google Alerts Grader: http://alerts.grader.com

Google Reader: www.google.com/reader

HootSuite: www.hootsuite.com

HubSpot Article on Facebook: www.slideshare.net/HubSpot/a-visual-guide-to-b2b-facebook-pages-4277600

Mashable: www.mashable.com

Netvibes: www.netvibes.com

Sprout Social: www.sproutsocial.com

TechCrunch: www.techcrunch.com

Tweetadder: www.tweetadder.com

Tweetscan: www.tweetscan.com

Twellow: www.twellow.com

Twhirl: www.twhirl.org

Twitalyzer: www.twitalyzer.com

Twitterfeed: www.twitterfeed.com

Monitoring Social Media

Addict-o-matic: www.addictomatic.com

BoardTracker:www.boardtracker.com

FriendFeed: www.friendfeed.com

HowSociable?: www.howsociable.com

Icerocket: www.icerocket.com

SamePoint: www.samepoint.com

Socialmention: www.socialmention.com

UberVU: www.ubervu.com

PR

Daryl Wilcox white papers: www.dwpub.com/whitepapers

Free Publicity eBook: www.ihubbub/eBooks

Media centre URL example: www.ihubbub.com/press-office

Newspaper Licensing Agency: www.nla.co.uk

Online Dictionary: www.dictionary.com

Online Thesaurus: www.thesaurus.com

Press Release Layout: www.prweb.com/pr/press-release-tip/anatomy-of-a-
pressrelease.html

WordWeb Pro: www.wordweb.info

Online Press Kits

Google sitemap: http://www.google.com/support/news_pub/bin/
answer.py?answer=74288

InstantMediaKit.com: www.instantmediakit.com

MediaRoom: www.mediaroom.com

onlinePressKit 24.7: www.presskit247.com

Media Contacts

Cision: www.uk.cision.com

Featuresexec: www.featuresexec.com

Magatopia: www.magatopia.com

Mediafinder: www.mediafinder.com

Media Requests: www.ihubbub.com/media-requests

PR Service: www.ihubbub.com/ihubbub-pr

Responsesource: www.responsesource.com

US Media Alerts

Blogger LinkUp: www.bloggerlinkup.com

Haro: www.helpareporter.com

PitchRate: www.pitchrate.com

ReporterConnection: www.reporterconnection.com

Reporter's Source: www.reporterssource.com

Distribution

Daryl Willcox Publishing: www.dwpub.com/submit

Get2Press: www.get2press.co.uk

PR Web: www.prweb.com

PR Web (UK): www.prwebuk.com

Awards

Awards Intelligence: www.awardsintelligence.co.uk

Boost Marketing: www.boost-marketing.co.uk

iHubbub's Media Calendar: www.ihubbub.com/get-media

Remote Worker Awards: www.remoteworkerawards.com

Email Marketing

Email Marketing Solution Providers

UK

GetResponse: www.getresponse.com

GraphicMail: www.graphicmail.co.uk

US

Aweber Communications: www.aweber.com

Infacta: www.infacta.com

MailChimp: www.mailchimp.com

SimplyCast: www.simplycast.com

Spam Checks

Spam Haus: www.spamhaus.org/definition.html

Spam Haus Blacklist: www.spamhaus.org/faq/answers.lasso?section=marketing%20faqs

About the Expert Panel

Toby Beresford, Pailz

Business: Pailz

Website: www.tobyberesford.com

Type of site: Social Media Expert

Blog: www.gamificationofwork.com

Twitter: @tobyberesford

Toby is a web applications entrepreneur with a slew of web projects to his name: from NHS telemedicine for faster skin complaint diagnosis in the late 1990s, to playing Facebook quizzes about your online friends for Sony PlayStation in 2010. Having sold Nudge Social Media in 2010, his current business Pailz is using social game mechanics to improve team communication.

Ross Jackson, Ross Jackson Consultancy

Business: Search Consultant

Website: www.rossjackson.co.uk

Type of site: Consultancy

Ross has been an internet marketing specialist since 1998. He has always believed that a website is no use to anyone unless it has targeted visitors. He has focused on search engine marketing (both SEO and PPC), and website conversion throughout his career. Over the years, Ross has worked with an enormous variety of organisations, from the very largest multinationals to the smallest one person outfits. He has managed multimillion pound AdWords campaigns, optimised many websites to the top of the organic listings, and trained hundreds of people in how to best go about promoting their own sites. Ross's motivation and primary focus for the service he provides is to 'turn searchers into visitors, and visitors into customers'.

Ian Dodson, Digital Marketing Institute

Business: Digital Marketing Institute

Website: www.digitalmarketinginstitute.co.uk

Type of site: Digital Marketing Training

Blog: digitalmarketinginstitute.ie/blog-post

Twitter: @dmigroup

Ian Dodson is joint CEO of the Digital Marketing Institute, Ireland's leading professional body for the digital marketing industry. He has worked in e-business for 12 years with organisations such as Oracle Consulting and WebKitchen. He works with leading brands and organisations on the implementation of digital strategies. He is a prolific writer and speaker on all matters digital.

Judith Lewis, Beyond

Business: Beyond

Website: www.decabbit.com

Type of site: Integrated Marketing Agency

Twitter: @judithlewis

Judith comes from a technical background and has extensive experience in performing 'hands-on' SEO. She indulges in everything from keyword research through to content development and link building. Judith has worked strategically for clients including Fidelity, GalaCoral, the National Gallery, NBC Universal, *Reader's Digest*, Bayer, RBS & NatWest, the CIPD, Orange and the COI (UK Government), creating integrated strategies involving paid and natural search combined with social media marketing. Judith heads up a specialist search team, working to deliver fully integrated digital solutions. She writes regularly for SEO Chicks as a blogger, Centaur's *Technology Weekly*, a B2B newsletter covering news around the internet and 'Mostly About Chocolate', where she writes about her other passion.

Anthony Quigley, WebKitchen

Business: WebKitchen

Website: www.webkitchen.ie

Type of site: Web Consultants

Twitter: @anthonyquigley

LinkedIn: anthonyquigley

Anthony is a leading online marketer and expert in all things digital. As founder and Joint CEO of Irish-based Digital Marketing Institute and MD of WebKitchen, Anthony is considered to be one of the pioneers of digital marketing in Ireland. Anthony advises and mentors organisations in how to plan and implement digital marketing campaigns, using online technologies as part of their business growth. Anthony's specialities include digital marketing, Google, social media networking and online marketing strategy development.

Dan Fallon, Search Star

Business: Search Star

Website: www.search-star.co.uk

Type of site: Google Advertising Professionals

Blog: search-star.co.uk/blog

Twitter: @Search_Star

Dan Fallon is Managing Director of Search Star. He started working in advertising after graduating from Warwick University where he studied economics. He has a

Chartered Institute of Marketing Diploma. Dan has worked in media agencies buying advertising (MediaCom, Manning Gottlieb OMD and The Response Team), starting as a Graduate Planner/Buyer and becoming a Media Director. He first bought advertising from Google in 2002 and immediately saw its potential versus other advertising media and focused his career and client budgets into search. In January 2005, Dan became one of the first people in the UK to qualify as a Google Advertising Professional and founded Search Star. Search Star currently has staff driving clicks, analysing results and optimising for their clients' profit.

Dee Blick, FCIM, Chartered Marketer

Business: The Marketing Gym

Website: www.themarketinggym.org

Type of site: Marketing

Dee Blick is a Fellow of the Chartered Institute of Marketing, the world's largest marketing body. Fellowship is the highest status that can be awarded to any marketer worldwide. In the last six years, Dee has won six awards for her press releases, adverts and media business articles. She is also a published author of the Amazon best-seller *Powerful Marketing on a Shoestring Budget for Small Businesses*. Dee also writes for a number of recognised brands including British Telecom, The Hamerville Publishing Group plus many other publications, including the *Financial Mail* Women's Forum and is a keen blogger. Dee was also featured as a marketing entrepreneur on the BBC alongside *The Apprentice* star Saira Khan.

Andrew Seel, Qube Media

Business: Qube Media

Website: www.qubemedia.net

Type of site: Social Media Agency

Twitter: @seelpod

Blog: qubemedia.net/blog

Andrew Seel is Managing Director of Qube Media, one of the original social media consultancies, and Director of ThePet.net, a leading social networking site for pet owners and businesses. He is a social media and marketing expert with over 15 years' experience in the digital industry and his social media experience goes back to the early days of the web. He has worked with AOL, LastMinute.com, Expedia, Black and Asian History Map for Channel 4 and Gorillaz animated band for EMI. He now runs social media collaboration strategies for clients such as Saatchi & Saatchi, Wall's, Virgin Atlantic and the Financial Services Authority.

Alex Johnson, Journalist and Founder of Shedworking

Business: Shedworking

Website: www.shedworking.co.uk

Type of site: Shed Working Blog

Twitter: @shedworking

Blog: junglecatmedia.com

Alex Johnson is the founding editor of Shedworking, which is devoted to the lifestyles of those who work from garden offices and other shedlike atmospheres.

Alex is a freelance journalist, part of the online team at *The Independent* newspaper, webmaster at Designer Breakfasts and an editorial consultant for several major charities. He is also a judge in the internationally acclaimed Shed of the Year competition. As well as Shedworking, he writes blogs about bookshelves and coaches Social Media for Junglecat Media and his book 'Bookshelf', based on the blog of the same name, will be published in 2012.

Fiona Wright, Journalist, Founder SchoolBuzz

Business: Journalist

Website: www.schoolbuzz.co.uk

Type of site: Parenting and school buzz

Fiona Wright has been a journalist and editor for national consumer magazines and newspapers for 20 years. She was Editor of women's magazine *Shape*, and has written and edited for titles including the *Daily Mail, The Mirror, The Daily Express, She, Glamour, Woman and Home* and *Good Housekeeping*. She has appeared as a media expert on *GMTV, BBC Breakfast* and *Sky News* and *LK Today*.

About Paula Wynne

www.suepix.co.uk

After a career as a publicist and marketer, Paula Wynne is now an award-winning online entrepreneur, women's ambassador, speaker and the bestselling author of *Create A Successful Website*.

She aims to help others work flexibly, as she has needed to do, and Remote Employment is her and her partner's vision for bringing a better quality work life to working parents across the UK. Completely inspired during the writing of her first book, Paula set about creating her and Ken's dream website – a social community for home-based working – and iHubbub was born.

Paula is also the organiser of the unique and popular Remote Worker Awards and is a SEEDA Women's Enterprise Ambassador as well as a mentor for online start ups.

Remote Employment won the BT Small Business Week 'Responsible Business Day' Award. Remote Employment was also nominated for the prestigious Barclays Trading Places Award.

Paula was awarded Karen Darby as her mentor in the FreshIdeas Events Mentor Competition, she was runner-up in the Enterprise Challenge of the Enterprising Women Awards 2009 and Finalist in the Best Online Business in the Women on their Way Awards.

More Praise for Pimp My Site

"Very well organised content. Packed full of great advice that has been learnt through past experiences. I can't wait to get started on our new website!"
Victoria Bell, Jan Constantine, www.janconstantine.com

"Full of tonnes of information and useful content. Paula's SEO tips are invaluable for your website. I really enjoy her teaching style as she engages beginners to get the most of their learning!"
Sarah Green, PA at Zircon Management Consulting Ltd.

"Wonderful and very helpful to hear SEO explained in such an easy to understand way."
Rhys Davis, Belts and Briefcases, www.beltsandbriefcases.com

"Very informative. After listening to Paula's SEO advice and putting her suggestions into practise on my website I have seen a great increase in traffic! In optimising my keywords, metadata and relevant link building, my site has become more efficient in bringing in more new visitors. I am so pleased to say Paula's SEO advice has definitely changed my website traffic!"
Mercedes Nagore, Stylemode, www.stylemode.co.uk.

"Paula's a blast! She knows her subject and I now have so much confidence. Her advice has given me an insight to SEO. I could listen to her for hours! Thank you Paula."
Juliet Can, Training and Events, www.trainingandevents.co.uk

"As you know with running a business you have to be a master of all trades, so I thank you for the great practical and useful advice. And for inspiring me!"
Rosie Hazleton, Wild Rose Escapes, www.wildrose-escapes.co.uk

"The way Paula gives information for a novice is very interesting and helpful and easy to understand. I am now really excited and looking forward to promoting my business with more success. Thank you Paula."
Igor Korenev, www.combit-services.com

"Paula's advice has helped me hugely to roll out an effective PR Strategy for my apartment business."
Susanne More, X-Ecosse Ltd, www.landmark-canary-wharf.co.uk

"Great advice with very practical, hands-on tips to get you started on the PR journey."
Madhu Rajesh, Business Development Director, Vital Regeneration, www.vital-regeneration.org

"Thanks for the motivating and highly informative information. Paula covers a lot of ground in a short time and answered all the PR questions that I had. I highly recommend Paula's teaching and I can't wait for more!"
Caroline Ainslie, Bubblz Maths, www.bubblz.co.uk

"Paula has exceeded my expectations regarding how to optimise my website and lots of PR strategy for my business."
Lucy Schoeps, Better Than Clean, www.betterthanclean.co.uk

"Very inspirational, valuable information disseminated and a world of knowledge on the PR industry. I recommend Paula's down to earth principles!"
Shirley Daley, Daley Import Export Agency, www.daleytrade.com

Index